Also available at all good book stores

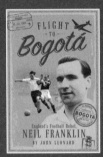

9781785316548

9781785316760

9781785314995

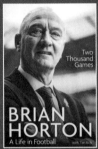

9781785316685

9781785316807

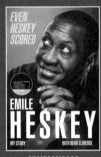

9781785315008

9781785316333

9781785317255

9781785315510

I'M WITH THE
COSMOS

I'M WITH THE
COSMOS

THE STORY OF
STEVE HUNT

WITH IAN McCAULEY

Foreword by Adrian Chiles

First published by Pitch Publishing, 2021

Pitch Publishing
A2 Yeoman Gate
Yeoman Way
Worthing
Sussex
BN13 3QZ
www.pitchpublishing.co.uk
info@pitchpublishing.co.uk

ISBN 978-1-78531-762-0

Typesetting and origination by Pitch Publishing
Printed and bound in India by Replika Press Pvt. Ltd.

Contents

This book is dedicated to my family, including my soulmate and wife, Kirsty, who has been an endless source of guidance and understanding.

Acknowledgements

A HUGE thank you to Ian McCauley and to Kathryn Dignan for their dedicated efforts with this project. Thanks also to Kath's brother, Patrick Dignan, for introducing me to Ian and Kath. Thanks to Mike Pearson, whose expertise with photographs has been invaluable. Finally, many thanks to Adrian Chiles for his kind words in the foreword, and to Paul and Jane Camillin at Pitch Publishing for their support.

Foreword by Adrian Chiles

I ONCE saw a beautiful thing at the Hawthorns. It was in the mid-1980s, when things of beauty were in short supply for West Brom fans, but this one would have shone in any era. I was standing behind the goal, about halfway back in the Birmingham Road End. I can't remember who we were playing. The penalty area was congested and one of our players had the ball on the edge of the area but instead of hammering it, hitting and hoping into the melee, he executed one of the most sublime chips I've ever seen.

The ball rose above the madding crowd before dipping under the crossbar. So it was that Steve Hunt imprinted himself forever on my footballing consciousness.

He already had an air of mystery, devilment and the downright exotic about him. He had started out at Aston Villa for a start, never something to commend a man to any West Brom fan. Even worse, he left us to go back to them, but I'll let that pass. And then there was the exotic something else of which we were dimly aware: his time in New York City with the Cosmos.

Blokes from Birmingham who had played for the likes of Villa, Coventry and us, generally didn't also have a stint with Pelé under their belts. What was that all about? For the teenage me it was quite difficult to get my head around, until the arc of that chip somehow made sense of it all.

It must have been 25 years later when his name came up at work. Steve Hunt! What on Earth is he doing now? Somebody told me he was working at a caravan park on the Isle of Wight. Now there's nothing wrong with working on a caravan park on the Isle of Wight, far from it, but it's not what I felt comfortable with for one of the finest players I had ever seen in my club's colours. I got to interview him on a radio show, but not for long enough to get the whole tale now told here.

Footballers' stories always enthral me, but they're getting slightly less interesting all the time. These days they're all rather similar: a kid is spotted at an alarmingly early age and then gives up much of their childhood for the chance of a career in the game. Heartbreakingly few make it but many of those who do trouser an awful lot of money in a short time before fading into comfortable obscurity. I don't begrudge them any of it, but stories like Steve's are more interesting than that. It's the story of a life in the sport told by a gifted footballer who played the game just off the shoulder of the household names, the legends even, we're all familiar with. His perspective is fascinating.

I have to tell you I wasn't Steve's first pick to write this foreword. His first choice was Pelé, which is fair enough. It's quite an honour to play second fiddle to Pelé, and even more of an honour to write these words for Steve. Enjoy his story.

Introduction by Ian McCauley

A Shaft of Light

In the 1971/72 season, Aston Villa were in the third tier of English football. It was an ignominious position for a club with such a distinguished history. It was also a depressing period for their supporters, which is perhaps why they responded with such enthusiasm to the news that the world's greatest player, Pelé, was going to grace Villa Park. Although the old stadium always had an air of grandiosity, much resented by city rivals Birmingham City, the ground still retained the Witton End terrace, which was no more than a mound of earth into which concrete steps had been inserted. There was no stand.

For modern players and supporters, it is impossible to convey first-hand how exalted Pelé was. He transcended the game in much the same way that Lionel Messi does today. The difference was that the English public had been denied regular access to Pelé's genius. He had been crudely treated by opponents in England during the 1966 World Cup. Today, we can watch Messi's club football live on TV, he can be seen in England at Champions League games, and we marvel at his genius over and over again on YouTube. We had watched Pelé in World Cups but he played his club football in Brazil for Santos.

By this time, Santos, with their world-class players, and with Pelé as the main attraction, were like the Harlem Globetrotters. Keen to cash in on the great Pelé, Santos had been playing a series of exhibition friendly matches in Europe for many years. Aston Villa supporters were unworried by the commercial aspect of this fixture; all they knew was that they had a once-in-a-lifetime opportunity to see this genius live at the grand old ground.

Some 55,000 Brummies gathered at Villa Park. The country was in the midst of the miners' strike; Villa were in the Third Division. Why wouldn't anybody want to lighten the gloom? For people who didn't have the opportunity to see Pelé play, this report from *The Times* gives a sense of his brilliance, 'Trying to contain Pelé is like trying to capture a shaft of light in a matchbox. At one moment he looks as harmless as a sleeping cat. The next he has disappeared into open space with feline speed, sliding past man after man so that they are left in a maze looking for the ball.'

Santos played as if it were an exhibition game, whereas Villa were eager to gain a notable scalp. Villa won 2-1 but the result didn't really matter. Pelé was playing at half-pace, but still produced a range of flicks and feints, and a range of passing that produced excited gasps from the Brummies in the crowd. He was given a rapturous reception, the Villa fans chanting his name, and constant appeals were made for fans to climb down from the floodlights (which incidentally failed at one point, holding up the match).

At the end of the game the crowd was ecstatic, not because Villa had won but because they could say that they had seen the great Pelé in the flesh. They could boast about the day they saw the best footballer on the planet.

One Birmingham boy of 16, however, would soon trump that. He was an apprentice at Villa on that day and had his photograph taken with the great man. Born and bred within spitting distance of Villa Park, five years later he could truthfully state that Pele was his teammate. This is the extraordinary football story of that Birmingham boy.

He's Behind You

On 28 August 1977, in the 19th minute of the game between New York Cosmos and Seattle Sounders, Steve Hunt scored one of the most memorable goals in his career, and one of the most important in American Soccer Bowl history. Look closely at the footage and you will see a wonderful pass from Giorgio Chinaglia with the outside of his left foot. You will then see a determined run from Steve. The ball, however, was gathered by the goalkeeper, Tony Chursky. Steve had outpaced the full-back and just failed to make it – his run had taken him beyond the goal line and Chursky had gathered the ball. Did Tony forget that Steve was still there? He seemed to take a glance. Did he see Steve and just not reckon on his pace and determination?

The keeper rolled the ball to his left, by which time Steve had sensed what was possible. The keeper had his back to him. One of Tony's Seattle team-mates was shouting, warning Chursky that Steve was behind him. By the time the keeper had realised the danger Steve had nudged the ball with his left foot. A futile race to the line ended with the keeper rugby-tackling Steve, but that little nudge with his left foot was history.

Steve runs away with one arm aloft to be held in the embrace of a beaming Pelé – the superstar he had been thrilled to be photographed with at Villa Park. This was Pelé's last game of competitive football: the Soccer Bowl Final between New York Cosmos and Seattle Sounders. 'We all felt responsible,' said Steve. 'We wanted to do it for Pelé.' This wasn't Steve's only contribution to the great

Brazilian's last game. He produced a perfect left-footed cross for Chinaglia to head powerfully for the winning goal as Cosmos came out 2-1 victors. Pelé's joy at the triumph was unconfined. It meant a lot to him. 'After three World Cups – now this!' he beamed. 'I can stop now, as a champion. I can die now. I have everything I wanted from my life in soccer.'

Football as we know is a team game, but the man of the match – the most valuable player – was Steve Hunt. The first goal in the game was a tribute to Steve's determination; the second to his brilliant left foot. How did this young man, with only seven first-team appearances for Villa, find himself on the same team as Pelé, Chinaglia, Alberto, and Beckenbauer?

1

Freddie's Head

'USE BOTH feet, Steve.' That's what Uncle Dave and Uncle Den would say to me in the back garden of my nan and granddad's house at Brantley Road. It was good advice, but I knew it was my left foot that would do most of the work. Brantley Road was a terraced house with a long, thin garden. In front of a bedroom window was a home-made goal, built from three pieces of wood and a net.

Brantley Road was the hub of my life. Uncle Dave and my mum still live there. Brantley Road is in the shadow of Villa Park and we were a Villa family. My nan, Rose, had a season ticket, and it was with my mum and uncles that I went to Villa Park. Nan could only be described as a Villa fanatic. When Villa lost she had a habit of locking herself in the toilet, and it was difficult to console her. My granddad (Dimple) would stay at home to watch the wrestling and practise the moves – Nan told me not to encourage his

19

'grappling'. Strangely, Dimple wouldn't go to first-team games, but would go to watch Villa reserves.

Brantley Road was Evans family territory. My mum's sister, Bet, who was a lovely and kind woman, lived opposite our family home with my three cousins, Darren, Julie and Jason. My nan, granddad and my mum's brother, Dave, also lived in the road. Dave still lives in the house he was brought up in, and my mum returned to Brantley Road to move into the flat that my cousin had vacated. Uncle Den and Aunt Lin moved to Great Barr with my cousins Paul and Joanne. Aunt Bet and Uncle Ron later moved even closer to Villa Park; it resulted in a comical moment during a reserve game – more details to follow in the next chapter.

I was pleased when my mum moved back to Brantley Road, as she is very close to my Uncle Dave, but the community spirit of the street has been lost. When I was a kid, council estates were respectable places; there were high standards and a sense of respect among the residents. Unfortunately, although of course there are still a lot of decent people living in the area, it is simply not the same. Last month, my mum and Dave went to Weymouth for a holiday and returned to find that a load of rubbish had been dumped in Mum's front garden. I know I sound like an old man saying 'things ain't what they used to be', but it makes my blood boil when an elderly lady can't go on holiday without someone taking advantage of her absence.

I now live on the Isle of Wight – more of which later – but suffice it to say that I have very happy memories of family holidays here on the island, where a ball was never far from my feet. Some sort of yearning for childhood innocence may have been a factor in my desire to live on the island.

When I moved with my mum and dad to Perry Barr, after a previous move to Nechells, it was to the tenth floor of a tower block. At the time it seemed exciting moving to a tower block, but I can see why people said they were totally unsuitable for young families, especially when the lift didn't work. You do wonder why the town planners didn't anticipate the problems. My mum, though, actually loved the flat.

When I moved to America, Rose moved in with her. She was virtually bed-ridden so it must have been a difficult period for my mum, as she had given up her job at the *Birmingham Evening Mail*, where she made the tea. The position provided her with an outlet and I think she enjoyed that social contact. The sports reporters would often ask her for bits of gossip from Villa Park in my first spell at Villa, things like, 'What does Steve think of the latest signing?'; 'What's the team going to be next Saturday?'

After giving up her job, and while looking after Nan, I think my mum felt isolated. I was in America experiencing problems of my own and trying to focus on football, but when I think back, perhaps I should have been more aware of her isolation in that tower block – though I think she would agree that I have been a good son. Besides which, my mum, in the stoic manner of so many women of that generation, tried to conceal what she was going through. It is certainly the case that my return to England was, at least in part, because I wanted to be near her. Cosmos offered me a good contract but I was determined to keep an eye on her, and help in any way I could. She is a strong and proud woman; I am glad that my football career largely took place in the West Midlands, and family is still the most important element in my life.

My mum was always there for me, providing total support for my football and every other aspect of my childhood. I was an only child but my mum, nan, granddad, uncles and aunts always made me feel part of a large, loving family.

It is strange in this modern era of football academies, when children are scouted at five or six, to remember that the trajectory of footballers in my time was quite different. In many ways, the path of my career was quite conventional for the period: a football-mad boy playing in the back garden; a loving mum who supported my football; playing for my primary school, Yewtree, encouraged by Mr Salt, our PE teacher who urged us to 'have fun' when playing. At the age of 11, I signed for Stanley Star (Villa Boys). I went on to play for Aston Boys and the Warwickshire county side.

We were a football family. Uncle Dave still turns out occasionally for Brantley Rovers, the side he founded, and also loves walking football. It may seem a little strange that I haven't mentioned my dad, after all most football-mad kids are encouraged by football-loving fathers. I do remember seeing my dad play, but his influence on my life and my football was minimal. The last time I saw him was when I was 16.

I don't make close friends easily, but Dean has been my friend since the age of five and remains my closest friend. Dean and I grew up in Brantley Road, and both of us moved with our families to Perry Barr – in my case when I was 11. We both attended Great Barr Comprehensive and, although we were in different years, we were pretty well inseparable as kids. Dean probably spent more time at our place than at his own. We bonded through music and football. Often, we would be playing music in my bedroom where, from the window, a red light would flash. Mum rarely asked me to turn the music down, except when we played Jimi Hendrix, but she wasn't very happy about the red light. I think she thought it might be misinterpreted.

In those days my dad would come straight home, put his suit on, and, as quickly as he could, go to the local working men's club. To be perfectly frank, I preferred it when he went out. There was always an atmosphere when he was at home, and there were regular arguments between my dad and my mum. I suppose I have always felt defensive of my mum. She has been a constant support, and probably one factor in why I haven't made contact with my dad. Anyway, life seemed calmer when he finally left for good.

My interest in music was always there, but one particular gig changed my life. Uncle Dave took Dean and I to see The Who in 1969, and it felt like pure escape; the energy of the band seemed to penetrate your skin and overwhelm your senses. I knew from that moment that music would be a constant in my life, and I could tell that Dean felt the same. Dean and I went to gigs every week. I remember particularly seeing Curved Air, Jethro Tull, Free, Led Zeppelin, and the Rolling Stones. The usual venue for big gigs was the Town Hall, most often with Dave, who, with typical generosity, would buy the tickets. Occasionally we would go to Henry's Blues House. At these gigs, it felt that we were entering a world far removed from inner city Aston and the tower blocks of Perry Barr.

I have a lot to thank my uncles for as not only did they introduce me to live music, they were always encouraging my football. They were quite different characters. Uncle Dave is in his 70s now and to the best of my knowledge has never used bad language, had an alcoholic drink, or smoked a cigarette. One of the reasons he stopped going to Villa Park was because he got sick of the swearing. Den, who died in his 50s, was very different; he had been in the army, and if he heard someone on the terrace criticise me he was fierce in his determination to defend my corner. Den in some ways prepared me for the practical jokes that footballers tend to favour; he put cornflakes in my bed, superglued my bedroom door shut, and on one occasion, inserted a clothes peg in a sausage, killing himself laughing as I bit into it. They played together for Brantley Rovers, the team Dave formed with friends in 1963; Dave was a midfield player and Den was a centre-half. If an opponent clobbered Dave you could guarantee Den would put his foot in on the perpetrator.

Dean and I played football together throughout our childhood and teens. We would play one-on-one in the concrete pedestrian subway of Perry Barr, sometimes using the entrance as a goal. I learned a lot of my dribbling and shooting skills in that subway, and it has to be said that Dean wasn't a bad goalkeeper.

It is said that Pelé began playing football using a sock stuffed with paper. Dean and I had a ball, but Pelé was 16 years older than me, and I can imagine that kids might have been kicking socks filled with paper on the back streets of Aston during the war. Football is universal. Pelé describes football as more an obsession than a pastime, and I guess that's the way it was for me. I wasn't much interested in academic subjects. From my classroom windows I could gaze at the goals on the local recreation ground next to the school. In my classroom daydreams I would see myself curling a free kick over a wall into the corner of the goal. My mum made me do my homework, and I was no trouble at school, but I just couldn't wait to get out with a ball – usually with Dean. We would go out in all weathers. I was a professional footballer for 14 years, but I still count those days innocently kicking about with Dean as among the happiest memories of my football life.

In Mike Brearley's book, *On Form*, he writes about how the New Zealand Test cricket captain Brendon McCullum tried to emphasise the play aspect of professional sport by reminding his team about the innocent way they came to love cricket as kids. He urged his team-mates to recapture that spirit. As a boy I loved football, and I know exactly what Brendon meant. I guess, however, that capturing that spirit becomes more difficult when your living depends on playing a game. One footballer who always seems to transmit an innocent love of the game is Wayne Rooney. As I write he is with Derby County in the Championship, and despite Derby's poor form he still seems in love with playing the game that has provided the canvas for the expression of his rare gifts. Not least among these gifts is Rooney's football intelligence. Rooney has been a great player and he still doesn't get full credit for his achievements.

Dean and I did the normal things that teenagers do, including a bit of mischief-making. We used to attach wire to coins. We would then hide behind a wall, and, as an unwitting passer-by bent down, we would whip them away. Invariably, the hoax would result in us being chased through the back streets. We had to get the money back because it was the only pocket money we had.

I saw my dad play football once. He was left-footed and had a bit of pace. In my memory he was quite similar to me in his style of play. I am at a loss about why he took such little interest in my football; after all, most fathers would take pride in a son on the brink of the professional game. He was very interested in boxing and once bought me a Freddie Mills punching bag, with Freddie's head on the bag. When we were out, or going away, my mum would put Freddie's head in the window to suggest that someone was in. I think the fact that Freddie was totally stationary meant that he would only have deterred the most stupid of burglars.

That bag was also used in what may now seem some immature horseplay. In fact, some readers may regard it in a slightly harsher light. Freddie's head was not a pretty sight: battered by my youthful combination punches, it was in a state of disrepair. One day, Dean climbed on my shoulders and attached Freddie's battered head to the top of his own. We then concealed our bodies with a long raincoat so only my legs and Freddie's head could be seen – I guess we were about seven feet tall. We knocked on a front door and as it opened I said, in a deep, 'scary' voice, 'We're here for the rent.' To the householder, it must have seemed that the rent man's voice was emerging from the belly of a seven-foot man. We scarpered pretty quickly.

Throughout my school years my focus was mainly on football, playing for Stanley Star and hoping to gain an apprenticeship at Villa. I continued to go to music gigs with Dean, whose parents were breaking up, as were my own. Most young men don't talk about their emotional life, and we never spoke about our parents separating. As I have said, the atmosphere at home improved when my dad left, but I suppose a psychologist might suggest that his departure had an effect on my development, and the fact that I find it very difficult to forgive people who I believe have done me wrong. But music has always provided a release and football a point of focus. When I was struggling, with issues connected to my enforced retirement from the game, music was where I sought and gained my escape.

I had a brief flirtation as a kid with Manchester United. I suppose the main reason for that can be summed up in three words: Best, Charlton, Law. As a young prospective winger I was thrilled by George Best. It seemed that here was a player who had everything, and in my eyes he will always be the equal of Messi and Cristiano Ronaldo. I played against George for Villa reserves in my first spell at the club. I think it was after he had returned to United following one of his disappearing acts. Best was my hero, and I remember being incredibly excited that I was on the same pitch as him. I found it hard to focus. Perhaps that experience helped me when I went to Cosmos, and I found myself playing with Pelé, Beckenbauer and the rest. I was always aware of the necessity of maintaining my concentration. I played against George when he went to America, and bizarrely I faced him on another occasion when he was playing for Nuneaton. It was a benefit game for that club.

Best was the equal of Messi in emerging with the ball from a tangle of defenders. He was a brilliant dribbler, but he could also see a pass, had an awesome range of passing and he was a deadly finisher.

Best had the dribbling skills of an old-fashioned winger – the ability to manipulate the ball in tight spaces. Bobby Charlton wasn't a manipulator of the ball – his genius was when he had a bit of space ahead of him. He was quick and had a miraculous swerve which would take him clear of defenders. He also had that thunderbolt shot. I will always be a Villa man, but these two were my inspirations.

I played against Best in America but also in his time at Nuneaton, who had a £40,000 tax bill and Best was approached to play against Coventry as a means of making money with which to settle the payment. Typically, Best arrived with an ex-Miss World – Mary Stävin. It was during an alcohol-free period in his life, and he was absolutely brilliant, helping Nuneaton to a 2-1 win. I also played with Charlton in a testimonial for Phil Parkes, the Wolves keeper.

The other player I enjoyed watching in that United side was of course Denis Law. Let me leave the description to George Best, 'Denis was the best in the business. He could score goals from a hundredth of a chance, never mind half of one.'

I am very proud to have played with the superstars of Cosmos, but Best and Charlton were my heroes and I cherish the fact that I shared a pitch with them.

2

The Ron Saunders Charm School

MY DAD left home in the year that I first met Pelé. When Pelé played at Villa Park in 1972 he agreed to have his photo taken with me and two other Villa apprentices. I was thrilled to have met him and to have been photographed with him. The very idea that I would, for one season, play in the same team as him belonged in the realms of fantasy.

My mum was instrumental in me gaining my apprenticeship at Villa, although it was nearly aborted before it had properly begun. I had been assured verbally that I would get an apprenticeship when I reached the age of 16. These childhood dreams were nearly shattered when Neville Briggs, the chief scout, delivered a letter telling me that my place had gone to a boy from Sheffield, and that I would not in fact be signing for Villa. Briggs simply posted the letter through the door. I probably wouldn't have been any less devastated but I have always resented the fact that he didn't have the courtesy to speak to me or my mum before handing us the letter. I had been promised an apprenticeship, and I have never seen my mum quite as furious.

My mum worked in the same *Birmingham Mail* office as the father of Vic Crowe, the Villa manager, and he suggested that she should ring his son up while assuring her that this rejection would not be down to Vic. She followed this advice, and phoned Vic to make an appointment. With a sense of burning injustice, that perhaps only a loving mother can feel, my mum marched me to the manager's office and she demanded that the original promise of a place was honoured. I am sure that Mr Crowe recognised that I had been badly treated, but in conceding to my mum perhaps he recognised a force of nature that couldn't be resisted. Anyway, thanks mum.

Clearly Mr Crowe had made his feelings known to Mr Briggs, because we bumped into Neville on the way out. 'You nearly cost me my job,' he told my mum. 'Good,' was my mum's succinct reply. One happy outcome of my mum's success was that Villa provided her with a weekly allowance of £8 to buy steak. The thinking I suppose was that steak would 'build me up'. I was less keen on the raw eggs that they told her to give me.

During my formative years at Villa the under-18 side was very successful. In 1973 we won the Southern Cup by beating Ipswich over two legs. I scored in the second of those matches. Under Frank Upton, we won tournaments in Germany, Zambia and Holland. I later worked with Frank when I was coaching at Leicester, where he was the assistant physiotherapist. I went to see him about a stiff neck but I left the treatment room with a stiffer neck and in a great deal of pain. He was a much better youth team coach than a physiotherapist.

I have a lot to thank football for and these early tournaments gave me travel opportunities that would have been out of reach in any other job. It was astonishing for a young working-class boy from Aston to be in Zambia. We were near Victoria Falls, and I have just looked Victoria Falls up to find that it is the world's largest sheet of falling water. I must have been in a bit of a daze during that tour because I don't think I fully appreciated the geography. We won the tournament, but what I remember most vividly is a local newspaper stating that Steve Hunt 'crunched his studs unmercifully into an opponent's chest'. Unmercifully may be a bit harsh, but admittedly it was a bad challenge.

That Villa youth side contained some excellent prospects including Bobby McDonald, Jake Findlay, Keith Masefield and Alan Little. Ron Saunders, who succeeded Vic Crowe, got rid of all of us. Bobby was a terrific full-back who I played with at Villa and Coventry. He was the buccaneering type, and scored an astonishing 43 goals in his career. I was very close to Keith Masefield who made a career for himself with Arnhem in the Dutch league.

In the view of several members of the youth team, Saunders was a bully. Young players need to recognise that a certain amount of toughness is required to get to the top level, but some need nurturing. I never felt bullied, but when I needed encouragement, it didn't come. I can see now that his methods with certain personality types could be effective: players wanted to win his approval, and in creating that psychological dynamic Saunders built the title-winning and European Cup-winning side. He also indirectly provided me with motivation by selling me to Cosmos, and as I took the flight to America I was determined to prove him wrong and hoped I wouldn't cross his path again. I think I succeeded in the first part but unfortunately I did meet him again at the Albion.

Saunders, when he succeeded Crowe, immediately introduced a tougher regime based on physical fitness. The type of high-energy pressing football that Ron favoured required players to be in peak physical condition. He had the ability to motivate a certain type of individual and was a brilliant organiser. Unfortunately, despite his success there is rather more than that to being a manager of people, and in that capacity Saunders had huge flaws.

Mike Brearley, the former England cricket captain, writes in his autobiography about the importance of empathy in management. He gives as an example a story about sports coaches. A player has fallen into a hole; the first coach doesn't help him out, simply telling him he shouldn't have fallen into the hole in the first place. The second manager jumps into the hole with the player, and because he has seen people fall into this hole before he knows how to help him out of it. In my view Saunders was the first type. He lacked the empathy required to help players who had problems. In my experience, he was totally unsympathetic to injured players. He did me a favour in selling me to Cosmos, but not once did he offer me any positive feedback to cement a place in the first team. Young players need advice sometimes.

I have been watching *All or Nothing*, the documentary about Tottenham Hotspur in the 2019/20 season. When Jose Mourinho takes over the managerial job he explains that he only wants players who tune into his principles. He then goes on to say that he provides 'feedback without a filter', meaning that he will be frank about a player's performance. In my experience most players welcome this, but with Ron I really didn't have a clue what I could do to improve my prospects. In *Ticket to the Moon*, Richard Sydenham's book about Villa's European Cup-winning era, a quote from Allan Evans sums it up succinctly, 'If you were not in the first team, Ron didn't want to know you. "So what? So get in the first team."'

Young players need a mixture of encouragement and feedback without a filter. Ron's approach was effective with some players, but it was crude. He tried to intimidate young players into playing well, but he didn't have the empathy or insight to recognise that not all young players react in the same way.

Despite characterising himself as a manager who gives feedback with no filter, Mourinho emerges from the documentary as an empathetic type. In his first game at home, Spurs were 2-0 down to Olympiakos and he hauled Eric Dier off after 30 minutes. At half-time Dier's bearing was of a man who had just been sentenced to 20 years in prison. The following week Spurs were playing Bournemouth in a league fixture. In front of the camera, Mourinho explained to Daniel Levy his reasoning behind picking Dier for that fixture. He knew that Dier had felt humiliated by his substitution. He wanted to play him against Bournemouth, because it would give a much-needed boost to Dier and also for 'the feeling of the family'.

In the same episode, Mourinho is filmed talking to Dele Alli about the fluctuation in his form. He was trying to help Alli find a solution by encouraging self-reflection and analysis. Mourinho lets Alli know that he thinks he is a top player, but encourages him to examine why his performances had become inconsistent.

Saunders was a highly successful manager, but his treatment of Charlie Aitken provided more evidence of his lack of empathy. Charlie, one of the nicest guys you could ever meet, was treated abysmally by Saunders. He was Villa's record appearance maker, and at 33 he was forced to train away from Bodymoor Heath before joining Cosmos. It was my good fortune that Charlie did make that move because he had a large part to play in my transfer there, but Saunders's treatment of him was inexcusable. Saunders didn't like Charlie, and Saunders didn't like me. We both ended up 3,000 miles away.

My first game as a professional was for Villa reserves against Southampton reserves. I remember vividly my knee 'going' in that game and just as vividly recall the painful four-mile walk afterwards to my home in Perry Barr. I was hobbling, and in agony. The knee had not improved by the next time I reported for training. Saunders responded by suggested that I be taken for a long run along the driveway to Aston Manor; I lasted a few seconds before collapsing and was taken to Sandwell Hospital for a cartilage operation.

I am convinced that Saunders's fitness regime was partly to blame. At the core of training was an exercise that involved jumping two-footed over a series of hurdles. It was knackering, and I don't think it did our knees any good. In fact there was a spate of cartilage injuries at the club under Saunders. My return to fitness was further delayed when the physiotherapist attempted to take the stitches out. The physio was a man with certain liquid requirements; his unsteady hand with the scalpel caused a further two-week delay. I was a 17-year-old kid but I must say I received wonderful support from three experienced pros, Malcolm Beard, Geoff Vowden and Pat McMahon, who all came to visit me in hospital. Footballers often get a bad press but these were three of the good guys.

Bill Shorthouse, the reserve team manager, was a much more empathetic character than Saunders, but on one occasion he demanded too much. We were playing Liverpool reserves and my direct opponent was their much-feared hard man, Tommy Smith. I was a bit naïve; I went past him a few times before nutmegging him. I may have looked a little too pleased with myself when we were next in close proximity, waiting for a corner. Tommy pointed to the top tier of the stand. 'Can you see the top tier of the stand?' he asked me. 'Nutmeg me again and I'll kick you up there.' Shorthouse, having seen me go past Tommy, was baffled as to why I began to play one-touch football. 'Get after him! Take him on!' he kept shouting, which made it a relief when I moved to the other wing.

I mentioned earlier that my Aunt Bet moved close to Villa Park. She had a dog called Pluto who, on one evening, must have fancied a bit of a run about on the closest piece of grass. I was playing at Villa Park in a reserve game when the unmistakable form of Pluto came charging towards me as I patrolled the left wing. The referee was blowing his whistle as Pluto pursued me. I tried to pretend I didn't know Pluto, but I think it must have been apparent that he and I were old friends.

My debut for the first team came on 23 April 1975. I came off the bench against Sheffield Wednesday, and gloriously, it was the day Villa secured promotion to the top tier. As a Villa fan it was a wonderful feeling, and as a player I was inclined to think that with promotion secure I would have more chance of being selected for the following game. There was massive support for Villa at Hillsborough that day. We won 4-0 with two goals from Brian Little, one a brilliant virtuoso effort from 25 yards, one from Keith Leonard, and one from Ian Ross.

A photo I treasure is one from my full Villa debut in the following game. The picture shows me and my team-mates running out to a guard of honour from the Sunderland players. That photo captures the excitement that I felt. There I was, a childhood fan running out to play for my home club at a ground within shouting distance of my home.

When Saunders pinned up the team sheet and I realised I was making my full debut, naturally I was very excited. Perhaps I was overexcited, because I misunderstood one of Ron's instructions. On the morning of the day before the game, Ron was pressing his arms against the door frame of the changing room. It was a bit of a scary sight. I can remember the veins standing out in his arms as he said, 'Take the pill, son. Take it at one o'clock. It'll calm your nerves.' He handed me the pill, and I duly took it at 1pm that day. When I mentioned this to the experienced first team players they fell about laughing. Apparently, I was supposed to take it at 1pm the following day which would have been two hours before the game. Saunders found out and went ballistic. To this day, I have no idea what the pill was.

In his autobiography, John Burridge parodied The Crystals' 'Da Doo Ron Ron Ron', using it as the title of a chapter about Ron Saunders – so he ended up with 'The Dour Ron Ron Ron'. I wish I had thought of that. Ron was indeed a dour and hard man. His fitness routines were intense; each player was given 20 minutes of hard physical activity – jumping, twisting, turning, and clearing hurdles. On the plus side, if you avoided injury you were definitely fit. He used to say that if your cheeks were sunken you were fit. Villa's European Cup-winning side was fit and hard-running, and although they won it under Tony Barton, it was Saunders who had created the culture to enable that triumph.

Having made my debut, I did of course become better known in the city. This didn't stop Dean and I going into town on most Tuesdays for a drink. We would often meet other players, and I can honestly remember very few problems other than some occasional comments from Blues fans. In those days, it was much easier to mingle with supporters and be an integrated part of the city in which you lived; I should imagine today, with wall-to-wall coverage and social media, it would be well-nigh impossible.

When I was growing up in Aston, a few Villa players lived in lodgings on Brantley Road. The vast wealth that players in the Premier League enjoy today makes it difficult for them to live a grounded life, and I fear many of them will suffer the consequences. Their wealth will mean nothing if they do not have a focus when they retire. I am glad to see that the Duke of Cambridge is giving mental health in football a higher profile. It has been a long time coming.

Being on the fringes of the first team at Villa opened the door to a new world. One year, the first-team squad, including yours truly, went on a cruise to the West Indies.

Having spent a week in Barbados, we returned to the boat. Shortly after arriving back at our vessel we heard a huge bang in the engine room, which turned out to be an explosion that tore holes in the side of the boat. The reaction of the players will come as no surprise as the explosion resulted in a mass exodus to the bar where, with very few exceptions, they all proceeded to get hammered. When the lights came on we gazed over the side to see several hungry-looking sharks. Jim Cumbes, our goalkeeper, was also a first-class cricketer. He amused himself by throwing empty beer bottles at the sharks. I guess he needed the fielding practice.

John Burridge, aka 'Budgie', was at Villa in my first spell at the club. He was dedicated to getting the utmost out of his ability. I roomed with him before a game in Leeds and at 4am I was disturbed by heavy breathing. I looked across the room to see Budgie doing sit-ups. 'Got to keep fit mate,' he said. He then asked me to throw him an orange. I had assumed he wanted to eat it, but he told me that he wanted it thrown to the side. It quickly became apparent that he wanted to get some practice in. I spent ten minutes throwing the orange as he practised his diving on the full length of his bed. Budgie once invited me to a social do at his house. I arrived to see him leaping off the garage as some kind of training for his goalkeeping dives.

I went with the rest of the squad for a pre-season break in Martinique, where a young bloke was displaying his diving technique to a couple of pretty girls; he was full of himself and lapping up the attention, so we urged Budgie to put him in his place. Budgie walked on his hands, past the girls, on to the diving board and flipped off the springboard into the pool. The poser soon shuffled off, but this was the kind of stuff Ron Saunders hated. Budgie was a great bloke and totally dedicated, but sadly his commitment and dedication to football indirectly led to serious mental health issues. Happily he recovered. Budgie discusses these consequences with great perception in his autobiography. Later in this book, I will consider the effects of retirement on professional footballers.

Ron Saunders deserves credit for building Aston Villa's European Cup-winning team, but it is clear that he didn't fancy me as a player. This was confirmed later at West Bromwich Albion when he became manager. For most of the 1975/76 season I was in the reserves at Villa, but I did make my First Division debut against Liverpool in a goalless draw. I also played my first and last game in European competition, as a substitute, in the UEFA Cup against FC Antwerp. Little did I know that football was about to take me across the Atlantic.

The events leading up to my transfer to Cosmos were very sudden. I was preparing for an evening reserve game;

I was on the fringes of Aston Villa's first team, having been associated with the club since the age of 11, and had played seven games for the first team. A summons to Saunders's office came that afternoon. I knew it was something important. Direct and to the point, Saunders told me that there was a man in the Villa canteen who wanted to take me to New York Cosmos, and he added, 'I have accepted the offer.'

I had never heard of New York Cosmos, and was in a slightly confused state when I went to meet 'the man in the canteen'. There were two thoughts running through my mind. Firstly, New York was a long way away. Secondly, it was apparent that having achieved my childhood ambition, of running out at Villa Park as a member of the first team, it was now clear that the club I had supported and served my apprenticeship at was now willing to dispose of my services. Mr Saunders told me that the club needed the money from the transfer to provide funds to build a stand at the Witton End. To this day I call it the Steve Hunt Stand. Mind you, I'm the only one who does.

The man from Cosmos that day was Joe Mallett, the former Birmingham City manager, who at the time was coaching at the American club. 'I have never heard of New York Cosmos,' were my first words to Mr Mallett. Joe, a lovely man, persuaded me that I would be 'in at the start of a boom period in American soccer', and that they had chosen me over Tommy Hutchison (who I later played with at Coventry) because of my youth. Joe's next words probably clinched it for me, 'You'll have some interesting team-mates, son.' 'Who?' I asked. 'Well, there's a chap called Pelé. He can play a bit.'

The prospect of playing with Pelé was even more inviting than the fact that I was about to double my salary. I still had to talk this over with Sue, my first wife, who I had married only two months previously. Sue had an adventurous spirit and said that if I wanted to go she would come with me. The Cosmos years were about to begin but not before I had been bitten by a Rhodesian Ridgeback.

3

I'm With the Cosmos

Pelé and the Kaiser

On the evening before I went to New York I had visited a friend who owned a Rhodesian Ridgeback. I have always loved dogs, but on this occasion I came off worse from an ill-judged play fight which resulted in a badly cut ear. I arrived in New York with a bandage round my ear and looking like a Van Gogh self-portrait; it was not a great look for a meeting with my new team-mates.

In the film about Cosmos, *Once in a Lifetime*, the phrase 'I'm with the Cosmos' is used to convey a sense of glamour. Apparently saying 'I'm with the Cosmos' provided instant access to Studio 54, a glamorous New York nightclub. Warner Communications, the owners of Cosmos, did have a table reserved for Cosmos guests. I went twice. Studio 54 was an unlikely place for an innocent young man from Brantley Road to find himself. The club was at the centre of New York's bohemian social life and regular visitors included Andy Warhol, Liza Minnelli, Michael Jackson and Elton John. It was also patronised by an assortment of drag queens, transvestites and flamboyant figures from the New York gay scene. Most people on the dancefloor appeared to be completely off their heads. I did see a very elderly lady gyrating energetically, and let's simply say that her energy levels were unnaturally high; I later learned that she went by the name of Disco Sally. I have to admit that, even though it was quite an experience, I'm more at home in the pub.

Of course, I did enter a glamorous world of football superstars, and I met figures from the world of entertainment. Steve Ross, the boss of Cosmos and chief executive officer of Warner Communications, made sure he took full advantage of his contracted superstars to sprinkle more stardust on the club. Many actors, including Robert Redford, turned up in the locker room and at Cosmos functions and it was a great thrill to meet Mick Jagger and Peter Frampton.

There was, however, another side to that first year as the reality was that it was very far from glamorous for Sue. We had married shortly before the transfer to Cosmos. My first game was in Las Vegas, and Sue, at the age of 19, was stuck in a hotel – scared stiff of leaving the premises, and only exiting the room for meals. Even when we moved into our own apartment in North Bergen, New Jersey, we didn't venture too far; in fact, on a rare outing we got ripped off by a cab driver, and we were dumped on the wrong side of town to be confronted by a guy shouting obscenities. Of course, such things could have happened in Birmingham, but we were young, naïve and a little unworldly.

Most people at the club were welcoming and friendly, especially Joe Mallett and his wife Bertha, but I don't think a lot of thought went into how they could help us settle in a new country. Yes, the language was the same, although not many of the locals spoke fluent Brummie, but aspects of the American lifestyle were alien to us. I know that a lot of clubs these days hire people to help foreign players settle. They call them 'relocation consultants', not least because a player's form can be badly affected if he doesn't feel comfortable. Fortunately Joe and Bertha were very kind and empathetic people. They went out of their way to alleviate some of the problems we were experiencing. My new team-mate Gary Etherington was also incredibly supportive.

The world described in the film *Once in a Lifetime* did not entirely represent my lifestyle in the first year. Later, when we moved into an apartment in New Jersey, life became easier, but my contract reflected my status at the time I signed for the club, and we didn't even have a car.

There was a tension between the glamour I experienced at Cosmos and our rather isolated home life in suburban New Jersey. In some ways that first year was tough, but my good form ensured that I was in a stronger negotiating position for the second season when we had the use of a car and a beautiful apartment overlooking the Hudson River, and the club paid for Sue to travel on away trips. She enjoyed seeing different parts of America.

Charlie Aitken was at Cosmos when I arrived. It was Charlie who recommended me to the club. On that Las Vegas trip, Charlie's puritanical Scottish roots emerged. I was walking with Charlie and Gary Etherington along the main strip in Las Vegas when an open-top car pulled up and a young, blonde lady emerged to ask if we wanted a good time. Charlie clearly thought he was defending us against immoral forces and, acting as a barrier between me, Gary and the girl, promptly shouted, 'No! These lads have got a game to play.' I think my words to him were, 'I have got a mind of my own, Charlie.'

We lost in Las Vegas but beat Hawaii 2-1 in the romantically named Aloha Stadium. I often say, when asked why I moved to America, that the first two games were in Las Vegas and Hawaii rather than a reserve match at Bolton or Blackburn. This comparison is a little false because away trips in America were hard. You could be away for such a long time and it absolutely poured with rain in Hawaii. I would almost certainly have been drier after a reserve game in one of the forementioned northern towns. One bonus is that I scored my first goal to win us that match. And there was a sense of anticipation among the players because we had all heard rumours that Franz Beckenbauer was on his way to the club.

My first game for Cosmos was against Las Vegas Quicksilver. In the opposing team was a familiar face, Trevor Hockey. I had cleaned his boots when I was an apprentice at Villa. Trevor's boots always stuck in my mind because they weren't football boots, they were rugby boots. Trevor was an industrious player who liked to tackle – maybe he thought they suited his style of play. Playing alongside Trevor was the great Portuguese player, Eusebio. This was, I suppose, typical of American soccer – it was a melting pot where experienced British pros like Trevor played along with the superstars of the game. I was a bit of an odd one out because I was young and ambitious. It seemed a long way from Aston, as I enjoyed a drink in Trevor's Las Vegas apartment after the game.

Trevor had been a cult figure at Birmingham City with his long hair and beard. He was also a good player – the kind you wanted on your side. Like me, he started as a winger and moved to midfield. At Sheffield United he had provided the platform for Tony Currie to display his skills. The most successful period of his career was at Birmingham, but he also spent a year at Villa when I was an apprentice.

I have a vivid memory of Trevor and Bruce Rioch coming to blows in a first team v reserve team fixture at this time. These were two hard men, and they weren't holding back. I remember this fight so clearly because I was running the line. I didn't quite know what to do, after all I was only 16, and simply waved my flag haplessly. Vic Crowe, the manager, had been watching from the stand and appeared on the pitch to stop the fight. It was at this point that I realised that managerial authority is held intact by the narrowest of threads. They both told him in no uncertain terms to disappear, and carried on with their scrap. It seemed strange remembering this story in the exotic setting of Las Vegas. That evening in Las Vegas is a fond memory. Trevor was a good bloke, and he died tragically young from a heart attack at just 43.

Trevor was one of a select number of players to play for both Blues and Villa. Having played for three West Midlands club I have often wondered what I would have done if Blues had come in for me. I think that might have been a step too far and family might have lynched me.

Charlie Aitken scored very few goals – not surprising as he was a left-back who rarely crossed the halfway line, but it amused me to read in my Cosmos scrapbook that the 1,261st goal of Pelé's career was created by Charlie. An Aitken assist to a Pelé goal in New York. That was the kind of unlikely fact and statistic that American soccer provided. This was our first home game and I played a small part in the goal: a throw-in to Charlie, who passed it to Pelé. Pelé scored, of course; it was the second goal in a 2-0 win over Rochester Lancers.

Most people, understandably, ask me what it was like playing with Pelé. My memories of him off the pitch are of a gentleman with an easy manner. When I arrived at Bermuda airport I was wearing flares, a tank top and my hair resembled Ozzy Osbourne's. I was taken to the team hotel, where Pelé met me and was dressed immaculately in a lemon suit. I have often wondered what he really thought when he saw me with my bandaged ear and hippie clothes. Pelé was always immaculately dressed and I think he was one of the few men who could get away with wearing a pink suit, as he sometimes did.

He had such an engaging manner, and he welcomed me with a broad smile and put me at ease. After a game, Pelé would sign autographs for any youngster who wanted one. He had a wonderfully relaxed air off the park. Sometimes he was over-relaxed, and could fall asleep anywhere, often having to be tapped on the shoulder to be informed that the second half was about to begin. Sometimes I had to pinch myself when walking out on to the pitch with Pelé and Carlos Alberto. They had been members of the wonderful 1970 World Cup team. I remember seeing Carlos Alberto's stupendous goal against Italy in the 1970 World Cup Final: such a rocket finish from Pelé's pass after a nine-man move. He later said that, having played with Pelé for most of his career, they had a sixth sense of where each other would be. Like most people who loved that side I have strong memories of Pelé's 'misses': the brilliant attempt from the halfway line that went just wide and the extravagant dummy against Uruguay, when he ran around the baffled keeper and put the shot wide. Pelé was still capable of this kind of magic: he was a little slower maybe, but he could astonish you with his range of skills.

I was 14 when Brazil won the World Cup in 1970. Like most football lovers I was in awe of that team. Every young player must have been inspired by Pelé in that tournament. I forced myself not to bask in the glory of playing with him because I had a fierce desire to prove myself. Pelé and the others wanted to see what I had.

When I first went to Cosmos I could be hot-headed. In one game, Pelé had a go at me for shooting instead of passing to him. I don't speak Portuguese, but his tone suggested he wasn't happy. My reaction was to give him the finger. Childishly, I thrust a finger in each ear as he carried on with this tirade. I was soon given a lesson on the playing hierarchy. My number was instantly held up and I was substituted. Shep Messing, our American goalkeeper, compared my treatment of Pelé to the burning of the American flag. I suppose he was trying to suggest that Pelé had some sort of sacred status. I thought this was a ridiculous thing for Shep to say; two footballers having a row is hardly the equivalent of burning a nation's flag.

Pelé's fury when I shot instead of passing indicated that his competitive nature was still strong. In the foreword to *Rock 'n' Roll Soccer*, Ian Plenderleith's brilliant history of the NASL, Rodney Marsh confirms this, 'Off the field, Pelé was always the perfect gentleman, but on the field he would throw the elbow and harass the referee. He was not only the greatest player in the world but a proper winner.'

I have heard people say that Pelé's status in the game is overblown because, apart from at Cosmos, he played all his club football in Brazil where the standard wasn't as high as in Europe. Take it from me. Even at the age of 36 Pelé was of a standard few could hope to match. You only need to look back at the 1970 World Cup to be assured that Pelé deserved his status.

Here is more evidence; the man scored his 91st hat-trick in a game against Fort Lauderdale. He scored 91 hat-tricks!

If you don't think Pelé was an all-time great then I am afraid you don't know football. I have heard people make an argument for Maradona being a greater player than Pelé. Nobody could deny Maradona's quality. I am not convinced that Argentina would have won the World Cup in 1986 without him, and his achievement in taking Napoli to the Serie A title is the stuff of legend. All I know is that at 36 Pelé was still a wonderful player. He was a little slower, but he remained a fantastic finisher and had retained the natural elegance that characterised his game.

In that match against Fort Lauderdale I provided him with two assists. His third goal was accompanied by an avalanche of Frisbees spinning down to the pitch. A sponsor had given 600 Frisbees to young supporters, and again, I had to rub my eyes. Was this really me making the goals for Pelé? And prompting this avalanche of Frisbees?

As I write this, Lionel Messi has requested a transfer from Barcelona. I have heard it said that Messi is not what Guardiola and Manchester City require. It is said that Messi does not regain possession often enough, that he is no longer capable of pressing, and that, as it is City's defensive play that has been their weakness, Messi would not solve their problems. Messi is only 33. Pelé was 36 when I played with him, and not only was he still a great player, but I learned so much from playing with him. In my view, even at the age of 33, Messi would improve any side, and imagine what the likes of Phil Foden could learn. Messi has scored 25 or more league goals for over a decade, and he is the best passer, dribbler and goalscorer in the world. Ronaldo is now 35, and by all accounts has been superb for Juventus. Messi, in the Premier League, would be an inspiration for football-mad kids in this country.

Pelé could look after himself. He would remember bad tackles. Later, you would see him put his foot in against the guy who had previously kicked him, and he could also use his elbows on occasions. On one day, in a game against Washington, he channelled his inner Muhammad Ali.

On the Washington side was big Jim Steele, the ex-Southampton player with legs like tree trunks. I had annoyed Jim by saying that Washington were the worst team we had played after we had beaten them in a previous game, and, with characteristic gentility, he had responded by saying, 'I'm going to take care of Hunt. I'm going to fix him. We'll see how well he can run when he's horizontal.' Any excuse would have done.

After slipping to the deck after chasing a pass I stood up to find myself in the middle of a brawl. I am still unsure of the sequence of events, but Jim's clenched fists gave me an idea of his intent. Several other Washington players piled in. The next thing I knew, Pelé approached, throwing haymakers. When the referee finally restored a bit of control he pointed to the tunnel. I was in a state of confusion when he told me it was me being sent off. As I reluctantly went to walk off the pitch – after all, I was entirely innocent – the ref turned to me and then pointed to Pelé, 'Well, I can't send him off, can I?'

When I told this story to a cricket lover, he told me that W.G. Grace had once been given out lbw early in an innings. Apparently, he walked over to the umpire and pointed to the crowd, stating, 'They have come to see me bat, not you umpiring.' Of course, it was Pelé who should have been sent off, but the referee did have a point. Pelé was the undisputed main attraction. He later said, 'Sorry Steve,' and I'm glad to say that the sending off didn't come with a suspension. I think the film of the incident made it clear what had happened.

There is a curious precedent to this moment, which reinforces Pelé's status among football fans. Pelé describes it in his autobiography. It happened in Bogota in a game between Santos and the Colombian Olympic team. As Pelé describes it, the referee Chato sent off Lima, one of the Santos players. Pelé did not take kindly to this decision and made his feelings known. I saw him let rip a few times and he was not a shrinking violet. Unlike the referee who sent me off, Chato was not blessed with sound judgement, and perhaps he hadn't heard the W.G. Grace story. I don't think that W.G. is big in Bogota. Unfortunately for Chato, Pelé was very big in Bogota. Chato sent Pelé off, and a riot ensued. In Pelé's own words, the crowd 'were not going to let a referee spoil their day'. The police had to come on to the pitch to protect Chato, who was replaced. 'With the referee sent off, I could be unsent off,' was how Pelé viewed it all.

Pelé could clearly look after himself, but his minder Pedro was not the best at his job. I can't remember the game, but a man with eyes only for Pelé came on to the pitch. Pedro had sized up the situation and he bounded on to protect the great man. Pedro brought the invader down with a well-judged rugby tackle on the sandy inside of a baseball diamond. There was a cartoon melee of arms and legs partly hidden by flurries of sand. Only one man emerged out of the sandstorm, and it wasn't Pedro, who remained floored, dazed and confused. The invader ran over to Pelé, shook his hand, and left the pitch while the groggy Pedro tried to get to his feet.

It is Pelé's 80th birthday in the week I am writing this. It is nearly 50 years since I briefly met him at Villa Park, and 45 years since he welcomed me in Bermuda with his broad smile. I have been wondering what he thinks of what is known as 'the analytics revolution', through which clubs minutely analyse the performance of players and transfer targets.

In Pelé's autobiography he refers to the fact that before the 1958 World Cup, he – along with the other Brazilian players – was put through psychological tests to assess his mental strength. He was dismissed as lacking the will to win and was left out for the first two games. He was, however, selected for the quarter-final, the semi-final, and the final. He scored six goals in three games and was only 17 at the time. I would be astonished to find that Pelé lacked fighting spirit at any age. Those psychological tests must have been pretty flawed.

I can imagine Ron Wylie turning his nose up at all the analytical stuff clubs are so fond of these days; I can imagine him saying that he doesn't need an analyst to know a good player when he sees one. Dave Sexton, I think, would have given it a go. Jimmy Hill, the great innovator, would definitely have gone for it. Arsène Wenger you would have thought would embrace anything that might give him a marginal gain, but in his autobiography he writes about signing a player called Lamine N'Diaye for Cannes. He knew that N'Diaye's stats indicated he was a goalscorer, but Wenger wanted to see him play, and it was the close season. He arranged to meet him in a car park and took a few friends to have a kick-about. As soon as Wenger saw him play in the car park, he knew he wanted to sign him. This sounds more like Ron's style.

I became used to cheerleaders dancing on the touchline and teams being brought on the pitch in fire engines. When we played Portland Timbers the pre-match entertainment was a man sawing through a log, and I can remember a pianist playing throughout one game, speeding up and slowing down according to what was happening on the pitch. One Cosmos fixture, against the struggling Colorado Caribou, was notable for what I can only call an excess of razzamatazz. Pelé and the Caribou captain wore cowboy hats and arrived on the pitch on horseback, with the Cosmos line-up following behind. The height, or nadir, of pre-match hype occurred after Cosmos had won a first-leg play-off game against Fort Lauderdale Strikers. Before the return leg the Strikers emerged to clamber on the back of a fleet of Harley-Davidsons, to ride round the pitch with the local chapter of Hell's Angels. Following this unlikely procession was a hearse carrying a coffin. When the hearse finally stopped, Ron Newman, the Strikers manager, came out of the coffin saying, 'We're not dead yet.'

Playing for Cosmos was an education. Not only was I playing with great players but it was a different type of football. The emphasis at Cosmos was on possession, and training was structured around the idea that if our team dominated the ball with purpose we would invariably win. Our football was played from the back. Shep Messing would look to distribute it short to take advantage of our cultured defenders. It was also beneficial that our pitch at Giants Stadium was one of the better astroturf surfaces. It is easy to forget that at this time football in England was not played on the pitches we see today, and it could be difficult for a passing side to retain possession on a mud bath or uneven surface.

By the time Franz Beckenbauer arrived at Cosmos, Sue and I were living in North Bergen in New Jersey. We were missing home, but my game was improving. I was top of the assists, and I was about to play with another of the world's greats. If I close my eyes I can still see the Kaiser, effortlessly and deliberately scoring from a corner against Messing in training. The watching spectators broke into spontaneous applause.

The first thing I want to say about Franz is that he is a smashing bloke. My mum has never forgotten the Kaiser's hospitality when she visited me in New York. The Cosmos had booked a box at a stadium where harness racing took place. Franz was very kind, fetching my mum drinks and making sure she was comfortable. My mum has never forgotten that the Kaiser made a fuss of her.

Franz was so elegant playing for Cosmos as a sweeper or as a holding midfield player. He seemed to turn effortlessly on the ball, and I have never seen a player so accurate in passing with the outside of his foot. The Kaiser still had strong feelings about the World Cup Final of 1966. As a ten-year-old, watching Geoff Hurst crash the ball against the crossbar, I could not have imagined arguing with the great West German captain about the validity of that goal.

Kaiser, 'It was never a goal.'

Me, 'What was the score, Franz?'

Kaiser, reluctantly, '4-2.'

Me, 'Well, then, it was a goal, wasn't it?!'

It may not be widely known in the UK, but just as Henry Cooper was the face of Brut aftershave in the UK, so Beckenbauer was in Germany. This is how I came to be splashing on Brut, alongside Beckenbauer in the changing room at Giants Stadium, for a German advertising campaign. Bizarrely, in the course of this advert, I was asked to make 'panting noises' into a microphone on the pitch in an empty Giants Stadium; presumably I was expressing the pleasure of 'splashing it all over'. Franz was on film jumping and heading while I was off-camera, sweating.

Franz was an incredibly supportive presence who kept emphasising how important it was to keep your temper under control on the pitch. It didn't come easily to me, but even today I remember with gratitude how one of the legends of the game went out of his way to mentor a young unknown.

My mum has never forgotten Franz's kindness and nor has she forgotten her arrival at the airport in New York. A rather surly immigration officer was questioning her about the purpose of her visit. When she told him that she was there to watch her son play football, he looked indifferent until she mentioned that her son played for Cosmos. At that point his expression softened, and he waved her through with a smile. The words 'I'm with the Cosmos' could open doors; after all, Steve Ross was a very powerful man. No one was more aware of his power than his favourite player.

Dr Doom and Professor Destruction

Giorgio Chinaglia was a superb player, but he was not known for his modesty. As I have pointed out, I could be hot-headed. Giorgio had a lust for goals and like so many great strikers he could be selfish. I let him know what I thought of his selfishness, and he belted me on the chin. I wasn't the type to let that go and replied in kind. When this conflict had died down we had a chat and sorted it out. His job was to score goals. Apparently, mine was to make them for him.

As a goalscorer he was as good as anybody. His goal-to-shot ratio was unbelievable. Chinaglia had a huge ego, but when he said 'get the ball to me and I'll score' it was a statement of fact. He said the same thing to Pelé. Pelé thought that Giorgio tried to shoot too often from impossible angles. It was true. Chinaglia did try to score from impossible angles but I can't imagine, however, that any player scored more goals from those angles than he did.

When I went back to Cosmos in 1982 we had two talented lads from Paraguay: Roberto Cabanas and Julio César Romero. They had clearly not received the Chinaglia doctrine, 'Your job is to make goals for me.' We were playing Chicago, and Cabanas was one on one with their keeper. Giorgio was to the left waiting for a tap-in. It didn't come, but Cabanas scored. I thought that as Cabanas had scored even Giorgio might be pacified. I should have known better. In the changing room at half-time Chinaglia went absolutely berserk at Cabanas. It became physical. A full-on brawl erupted when Romero went to support his fellow Paraguayan, and the Cosmos team was divided into two warring factions. Chinaglia could have this effect.

Like me, Chinaglia had to leave home to prove himself. He had moved to Cardiff from Italy with his parents at the age of eight. He signed for Swansea as a teenager. There is a story in *Arrivederci Swansea*, the biography of Chinaglia by Mario Risoli, of how Giorgio, as an apprentice at the Welsh club, would resent doing the menial jobs that, in those days, were part of the rites of passage for aspiring footballers. Knowing Giorgio in later life, it does not at all surprise me that he thought he was above sweeping terraces or cleaning boots. When I was an apprentice at Villa, Alan Little had threatened to take me behind the stand when I refused to clean the showers again after he was dissatisfied with my first attempt. Giorgio was fortunate that somebody like Alan wasn't on his case. I can assure you he would soon have swept the terraces if Alan had been present.

Perhaps something profound connected to sweeping terraces occurred in Giorgio's psyche. I was told that in 1979, after I had returned to England, Giorgio took exception to a remark made by a man sweeping terraces at Giants Stadium. Apparently Giorgio then raced towards him and aimed a karate-style kick at him in the manner of Eric Cantona. Giorgio had seriously underestimated the caretaker's physical prowess and the man threw his broom down, having dodged the kick, and floored him with one punch. Equally Swansea had underestimated Giorgio's football ability when they released him. It was a decision that must rank, with the decision of a promoter to turn down the Beatles, as one of the most ill-advised ever made. He found a small club in Italy where he couldn't stop scoring, and eventually signed for Lazio where he became a legend and an Italian international. After our spat we had no further problems. I realised what an incredible goalscorer he was, and concentrated on my own game.

There is a newspaper picture of Giorgio and I celebrating my goal against Tampa Bay. Giorgio scored two that day. The heading is 'Doom and Destruction', and we are characterised as Dr Doom and Professor Destruction. I have done some research into Giorgio's character, Dr Doom. I note that Dr Doom, a Stan Lee Marvel comic villain, was blessed with diplomatic immunity, and it often seemed that, because of his relationship with Steve Ross, Giorgio had the same privilege. Apparently Dr Doom had a genius-level intellect. Well, I'm not sure that the comparison necessarily holds up thus far. I can, however, vouch for the fact that as a striker, Giorgio was a genius. I also note that Dr Doom had a substantial ego. It hardly needs saying, but so too did Giorgio. After that Tampa Bay game, Giorgio referred to his first goal, 'That was a beautiful goal, even if I do say so myself. I did it all on my own and was very proud of that one.' It was a brilliant goal. He had dribbled past two defenders and unleashed a typical Chinaglia power drive. Giorgio could have let his goal do the talking, but like Dr Doom he wasn't the retiring type.

Giorgio was a pure striker of the ball. He could make thunderous contact with very little back-lift. I have noticed that Harry Kane is similar in that respect. I learned where Giorgio wanted the ball played but the truth was that he could score from anywhere within shooting distance, and he was also brilliant at converting volleys. Chinaglia had been instrumental with Lazio in winning the Italian Serie A title in 1973/74, and he was top scorer in the league that season. On a European tour, a game against Grasshoppers Zurich was followed by a fixture against Lazio so we caught the overnight train from Zurich to Rome. I vaguely remember Giorgio bragging that his fans would be there to greet him. I took very little notice of his boasts until we arrived at Stazione Terminal, where we found hundreds of Lazio supporters waiting. I don't think I had realised the extent of Giorgio's celebrity in Rome; it seemed as though half the population of the city were waiting for him at the station. He was hoisted on somebody's shoulders and paraded through Rome's streets as a returning hero. Not bad for a Swansea reject.

Of course, receptions like the one Giorgio received in Rome fed what I can only describe as a narcissistic personality. Apparently he was also treated like a hero by large sections of the Italian community in New York. In *Once in a Lifetime,* Clive Toye, who had been general manager at Cosmos, tells a story about Giorgio arriving in New York to sign for the club. As Toye tells it, Giorgio had been sent an economy-class plane ticket to fly from Italy. According to Toye, Giorgio eschewed the economy ticket and hired a private jet because he had heard that Cosmos had done just that when Pelé arrived. I have no idea if that is true. Toye had an axe to grind with Chinaglia. The point, however, is that I wouldn't be surprised if this story was true. There was undoubtedly healthy competition between Pelé and Chinaglia on the field, but that rivalry was a driving force and was ultimately for the benefit of the team.

Giorgio and I were never going to be pals, but on the field there was mutual respect and we played well together. Like the great Vladislav Bogićević (more of him later), I became familiar with his diagonal runs. I had reason on the occasion of the game against Lazio to be very grateful to Giorgio after I scored the winner in a 2-1 victory. As I celebrated after scoring the goal, Giorgio came running towards me at full pelt. He was coming not to congratulate me, but to warn me, 'Stop! Don't *do* that. Stop celebrating. They'll kill you.' And he was deadly serious. I took his advice and it was easy to see that I had already angered the crowd. At half-time he put a protective arm around me as we walked off the pitch. It wasn't just the crowd I had enraged though. Giorgio insisted that I walked with him as we went out for the second half. The Lazio players were waiting in the tunnel. I had no doubt as to their intention and neither did Giorgio. 'Look straight ahead. Don't make eye contact,' he advised, as he again wrapped his arm around me. I was glad to finish the game and get off unscathed. I owed Giorgio.

Charlie Aitken suggested that Giorgio was jealous of my success at Cosmos, and Eddie Firmani once said, 'Chinaglia didn't get on with Steve Hunt.' I'm not sure if there was anything personal in it. Giorgio's career followed a pattern, if he was scoring goals he was happy.

Giorgio, not surprisingly, had a troubled retirement. He was charged by the Italian authorities with various offences linked to financial deception. By this time, he had become an American citizen, and after the charges he refused to return to Italy. As I say, we were very different people, but I'll raise a glass of his favourite tipple, Chivas Regal, to his memory. He died in 2012.

Giorgio was always happy to talk about his goals, but his tally of 737 does tell its own story. His nickname was 'Long John', supposedly after John Charles. If John Charles was better than Giorgio then he must have been some player.

It did not surprise me that Giorgio's life after retirement was dominated by criminal investigations into money laundering and fraud. His relationship with Steve Ross revealed a man who was essentially insecure. Giorgio wanted to be a big shot on and off the pitch and between 2004 and 2008, several arrest warrants were issued for Giorgio from Italy, but he stayed in America and avoided arrest. Poignantly, he only returned to Rome after his death to be buried in the city where he was a legend. It also doesn't surprise me that the Giorgio Chinaglia Foundation was set up by his children to help youth football programmes and disabled children, because this reflects the other side of his personality. He was a complicated man, insecure, with a huge ego, yet there are many stories of his kindness as well.

Sometimes, when I am doing some mundane task at the school where I am a caretaker, I think of the big man. We certainly went different ways. I think I got the best deal, but I don't think Giorgio would have been happy as a caretaker. In fact, he would not have been content being the headteacher – only Minister of Education would have been enough. Sometimes, in my mind's eye, I roll the ball into the path of his powerful stride, and marvel still at the sight of the ball nestling in the net before the goalkeeper has moved. Swansea City, you made one hell of a mistake.

The Scent of the Tiger

It has to be said that our form had improved with the arrival of Carlos Alberto in July 1977. What a player! He seemed to have a sixth sense. Like Beckenbauer, he made the game look easy, and his signing meant that Franz could play in a more advanced role. The transfer of Carlos made us a much more complete team and his arrival was a major factor in our qualification for the play-offs.

A crowd of nearly 60,000 gathered at Giants Stadium to watch us play Tampa Bay Rowdies in the first round of the 1977 Soccer Bowl play-offs. Rodney Marsh, who was playing for Tampa, had called Pelé the 'black Rodney Marsh' after Rodney had been asked if he was 'the white Pelé'. Marsh was a brilliant footballer but it was difficult to upstage Pelé. Pelé liked playing against Tampa. Maybe the good-natured banter with Rodney put him in the mood. The Eastern division play-off that season finished Cosmos 3 Tampa 0. Pelé scored two and Chinaglia one. I made three assists. If anyone is in any more doubt about Pelé, heed Marsh's words after that game, 'Pelé still amazes me. Even at 36 he can do things most of us dream of. He's simply amazing.'

An interested spectator that day was Giorgio Chinaglia's dad, Mario. It was a good job that Eddie Firmani picked the big man because I read in *Arrivederci Swansea* that, when Giorgio was left out of the Swansea team, Mario turned up at the ground with a meat cleaver looking for the manager.

The victory against Tampa took us into a two-game play-off against Fort Lauderdale Strikers. A new record crowd of 77,691 gathered at Giants Stadium for the first leg. We won, 8-3, and I scored two goals. Ron Newman, the Lauderdale manager, said, 'We pretty much kept Pelé out of the game but Franz Beckenbauer and Steve Hunt killed us. They were the stars of the game.' It was after this game that I met Mick Jagger, and another dine-out story from that match was that the goals were against Gordon Banks, who I had first seen play on that little TV in Brantley Road.

The strange thing about the play-offs was that the aggregate score did not come into play and an 8-3 victory meant no more than a 1-0. If the Strikers were to beat us or draw in the return leg it was shoot-out time. The shoot-outs in the NASL back then began on the 35-yard line. The goalkeeper could only handle the ball inside the penalty area, but he could leave it. It was a much more even contest than a penalty. I didn't like the shoot-out, and wasn't very good at it, although I never refused to have a go. It seemed to me that the keepers had nothing to lose. If they saved an attempt they were heroes; if it went in they weren't blamed. It was astonishing how many top players missed.

As you will see later in the book, I did sometimes make the mistake of delivering rash predictions. Take this, after the first game against the Strikers, 'We're so psyched, so confident now, that anything that gets in our way we're going to destroy.' So inevitably, after my prediction we played poorly in the return and Gordon Banks was brilliant. The game ended in a draw. It transpired, of course, that the game resulted in the dreaded shoot-out. I never felt comfortable during this one and it was a great relief when I scored the first goal to help us go through. Franz always advocated using the outside of the foot in a shoot-out, and I took his advice most of the time. I must say a word here about Shep Messing, because he was brilliant in that shoot-out, and saved two of the Strikers' efforts.

Both Pelé and Chinaglia praised Banks after the game, but in their own inimitable manner. I think these quotes give you an insight into their personalities. Pelé said, 'I played against Banks many times but tonight he was even better than in the 1970 World Cup.' Chinaglia, who scored the equaliser in open play, added, 'Hey! Banks held them in there all game, but it was Mr Chinaglia who got in there for the goal. That's 20 for the season.' That was Giorgio. Humility was not his defining characteristic.

The semi-final was against Rochester Lancers. Chinaglia and I scored in front of 20,000 at their Holleder Stadium. My goal was a gift as I was chasing a ball from Pelé when their centre-half and goalkeeper collided and I was left with an open goal. Again, Messing had an outstanding game, and Pelé's work rate was fantastic – a reminder that even for the greatest of players, working hard is the first obligation. We had to work hard and take the knocks because the Lancers were a very physical side.

Again, Giants Stadium was sold out for the second leg. Again, Mr Chinaglia got in there by scoring two goals in a 4-1 victory. We were on our way to Portland for the Soccer Bowl Final against Seattle Sounders, and the two moments that came to define my career in America.

There was a real sense of unity in the squad as we approached the 1977 Soccer Bowl. We were working with common purpose: everybody wanted to do it for Pelé. Even Giorgio was aware of the significance of the occasion, and wanted to win for the great man. The power struggles behind the scenes were forgotten and all that mattered was succeeding for Pelé. Julius Mazzei, the assistant coach who was Pelé's friend and mentor and who knew Pelé better than anybody, has since said that Pelé felt a kind of obligation to his legacy to win that game. The Seattle Sounders, however, were not there to make up the numbers. They had brought with them 12,000 of their own fans. *Soccer Corner* magazine reported that some visiting fans sported a giant bed sheet displaying the words, 'Cosmos: You Vill Lose and Like

It.' A message for Franz in less politically correct times. Don't mention the war.

My goal and assist against the Sounders have been described in the introduction, but my reaction when the Sounders keeper, Chursky, rolled the ball to his left and I beat him to it and nudged it in, owed a great deal to my observations of Pelé. He was always alert to any possibility of the keeper making an error. I have retained a description of the lead-up to that goal in *Soccer Corner*, 'Chinaglia has sent the speedy winger through with a long spinning ball that Chursky has gathered in by flinging himself sideways at the on-rushing Hunt. Then suddenly the Scent of the Tiger.' It was then that I took advantage of Chursky's error.

Football is not just about brilliant flashes of skill; it is also a game in which sharp awareness can lead to goals. Someone once said about Denis Law that even when the ball was at the other end of the field his eyes were always moving, taking the whole picture in and trying to visualise the potential sequence of events. I like to think of that goal as my tribute to Pelé's genius in that final game of his competitive career.

There is a picture of the moment after the goal which encapsulates the agony and the ecstasy of football. I am held aloft by Pelé and waving my left boot in the air. In the background is Tony Chursky kneeling on the goal line with the ball still nestled in the net. Chursky had played well, but, as has been said so often, if a goalkeeper makes one mistake it can define his day and even his career. 'Somebody had to be the goat today,' Tony said after the game. Mel Machin, who played for the Sounders that day, later said that when he saw me closing in on Chursky he warned him. Chursky didn't hear because he was deaf in one ear.

There were ten minutes remaining when it was announced that I was the man of the match, or as the Americans call it, Most Valuable Player (MVP). That announcement went straight to my head. I must have been intoxicated with joy and I decided to show everybody why I had been chosen. I picked up the ball in my own penalty area and recklessly decided to display my dribbling skills. I went past three players, but the fourth, Steve Buttle, nicked it. I owe Shep Messing. Buttle shot and Shep managed to tip it on to the post. In three minutes I had gone from man of the match to the man who nearly lost the game. I later learned that Franz was in despair when I went on that run. Half the team were shouting at me to boot the ball out. Thanks, Shep!

I will never forget the scene when the final whistle went. The Seattle players must have felt that their noses had been rubbed in it. The astroturf became the stage for a carnival of joy with even the press joining in, and everyone wanted a piece of Pelé. He was swept up and I don't think he touched the ground until we reached the changing room. From the changing room we could hear the crowd chanting his name. The entire Cosmos team picked up the singing and Pelé, an emotional man, had a tear in his eye. It must have been difficult for Seattle and for Chursky in particular, but the Seattle players were gracious losers. They were perhaps sad to lose but honoured, as I was, to be able to say that they played in Pelé's final game. 'God is very nice to me,' said Pelé, before adding that he could die a happy man.

One Seattle player left with a memento that is surely treasured to this day. As Pelé left the pitch he gave his shirt to Jimmy McAlister – a wonderful gesture to hand the shirt to the Rookie of the Year.

What also pleased me was that my goal in that game had similarities with my hero Best's disallowed effort in a game between Northern Ireland and England in 1971. Banks threw the ball in the air to volley it but before he could continue, George had deftly nicked it and headed it into an empty net. In my view it was a legitimate goal. George later said that he studied keepers and had noted mentally that Banks tended to throw the ball high before clearing.

My goal owed more to instinct and being alive to possibilities. I recently read an interview with Danny Ings, the Southampton centre-forward. He said that he also studied players and was aware of keepers and defenders who might be vulnerable to vigorous pressing. I admire his attitude. He made his debut for England in 2015 but didn't add to that first cap until five years later. He has been called up to the England squad in the week I am writing this, and he said that he had never given up on making more appearances. I was capped at the age of 28 and prior to that refused to give up on the dream of representing my country.

The cross for Chinaglia's winner against Seattle would have been the perfect finale. I had still not decided whether to come back, but after my fight with Chinaglia earlier that season, Giorgio's goal would have provided an appropriate conclusion to the year. As I said, when Giorgio told me, 'Your job is to make goals for me,' I started to understand his game – he simply lived to score goals. It occurred to me, however, that this might be the time to resume my career in England. This was before the intervention of Ahmet Ertegun, the president of Cosmos and founder of Atlantic Records.

'They Pay me to be Cool': Carlos Alberto

One great bonus of my years at Cosmos was meeting Ahmet Ertegun – a warm, kind man who knew I loved music. As the co-founder of Atlantic Records with his brother Nesuhi, and as a record producer and composer, he was a mine of music information. Ahmet had helped develop artists like Aretha Franklin and Otis Redding, and had signed Led Zeppelin and Crosby, Stills, Nash & Young. Ahmet and Nesuhi sold Atlantic to Warner Communications. Their enthusiasm for football was a major force in founding the Cosmos. Through Ahmet I met Mick Jagger and Peter Frampton. Ahmet brought Mick into the dressing room after the Strikers game when we won 8-3. All Mick wanted to talk about was football; as a big Stones fan, I just wanted to talk about music.

Ahmet loved his football, and I really enjoyed his company. After my first season at Cosmos I returned to Birmingham, and was undecided about returning to Cosmos or whether to try to prove myself in England. Eddie Firmani, the manager, was on tour in Europe with Cosmos, but that didn't stop him from ringing me regularly to try to persuade me to return to New York. I liked Eddie and was flattered, but it was a difficult decision. Both Sue and I had been homesick. It was probably harder for Sue than for me, but we had both missed family and friends.

I was trying to weigh these factors up when I received a phone call at my home in Birmingham. It was Ahmet, 'Hi Steve. I'm in London. Come and see me and bring your wife. I've got you tickets for the England–Italy game.' I explained to Ahmet that I was 100 miles away in Birmingham, and that it might all be a bit of a rush. 'No problem, Steve. I'll send a limo,' came the reply. That was how Sue and I came to be chauffeured to Ahmet's luxury London home, where Franz Beckenbauer was waiting with him. It was quickly apparent that I was wanted at Cosmos. I may be easily flattered, but with a music legend and the world's greatest defender in the room, and after gaining Sue's agreement, how could I refuse?

I did, however, want to negotiate a few improvements to my living circumstances. We had been housed in a small apartment in New Jersey and didn't have a car. We had both felt isolated. The football provided release and was a real thrill, but I think both Sue and I felt low at times in that first year. I would even suggest that my rows with Pelé and Chinaglia were partly triggered by the fact that we didn't feel settled. By the time I met Ahmet in London I had earned more bargaining power. I had enjoyed a good first season and wanted to take advantage of it. During the second season we lived in a beautiful rent-free apartment, overlooking the Hudson River, with spectacular views over the New York skyline. The club also provided a car and several free plane tickets to fly home and bring family over. I was worried about my mum, who was looking after my nan in that tenth-floor flat in Perry Barr. It was reassuring to have those plane tickets.

Ahmet was a generous man. One day he asked me if I needed any music, as I was always in the market. He gave me the number of his secretary at Atlantic Records, and suggested I ring her to make an appointment to view Atlantic's collection of vinyl. 'Take what you want, Steve,' he said. Excuse the cliché, but I was truly like a kid in a sweet shop when I saw the vinyl room. There were albums from floor to ceiling. I will always appreciate this wonderful gesture from Ahmet.

The post-Pelé era started much as the previous season had ended as we beat the Strikers 7-0. I scored three, as did Chinaglia. I had scored five goals in two games against the great Gordon Banks. I know that the sight in one of his eyes was slightly impaired, but it remains a feat of which I am very proud. He was still an excellent keeper, as evidenced by Pelé's comments after the previous season's second play-off game, although one aspect of his judgement was a little impaired. When Gordon was asked about me by the media, he compared me to a young George Best, saying, 'It's the way they both wriggle and jink on the ball.' It was hugely flattering because for me Best ranks with the game's greats. I think I deserved more than two England caps, but I was no George Best. Who was? But I am not too modest to

81

show the quote to anyone who wants to see it. Wouldn't you do the same?

After that 7-0 victory, Mick Jagger came into the changing room again. There was talk at this time that he was one of the owners of the Philadelphia Fury. In fact I understand that he had been involved, but had dropped out after receiving legal advice. His lawyers could clearly see the writing on the wall. Although over 44,000 attended that Cosmos v Strikers game there were already whispers about whether some franchises would survive. Two of the owners of the Fury were Peter Frampton and Rick Wakeman, and maybe their lawyers weren't as far-sighted as Mick's. I met both Peter and Rick, and for a fanatic like me, this access to rock royalty was a real bonus of playing for Cosmos.

Some of the football we played that season was fantastic. In fact, we seemed to be an even better side than before. Cosmos had signed Vladislav Bogićević (Bogie) from Red Star Belgrade, and we were now regularly attracting crowds of over 45,000. Chinaglia was still scoring goals, and Bogie made a hell of a lot of them. I produced my own fair share of assists and goals that season, but for a short period I struggled. I was being double-marked and man-marked. On one occasion against Seattle I threw my shirt down in frustration when I was substituted.

Eddie Firmani advised me to become more adventurous and move inside from time to time. Dennis Tueart, a top player, was also really helpful. Sometimes Dennis and I would switch, and I would become an inverted winger coming inside to get shooting opportunities on my left foot. In the meantime Chinaglia was gaining more and more power at the club in Pelé's absence. I am not sure Firmani had realised how far-reaching Chinaglia's influence had become.

My form must have improved because a Cosmos fan presented me with a t-shirt bearing the legend 'Soccer players do it for 90 minutes'. I made the mistake of wearing it to the players' bar where my colleagues told me that I wouldn't even get through the pre-match warm-up. One lady was clearly impressed by my shirt because she thrust a piece of paper in my hand. She had written, 'See you tonight for the 90-minute challenge.'

The team's form remained good; we were convincing winners of the league and had scored goals for fun. In the quarter-final of the play-offs we came up against the Minnesota Kicks and we would have been heavy favourites, but we lost 9-2. This hammering was a totally improbable result. The Kicks were excellent that day, and their English striker Alan Willey was on fire, scoring five goals. The standard of that performance was shocking but ironically it was Chinaglia who went crazy in the changing room, accusing us of complacency. After all, he wasn't known for tracking back. He must have had a word with his mate Steve Ross, because he later tore a strip off us, telling us that he was embarrassed by the performance. Ross's speech had the desired effect and we were highly motivated for the return, winning 4-0.

Just to remind you about the format, there was no aggregate score, and if both sides won a game each there would be a 30-minute mini-game. On this occasion the mini-game finished goalless, so it was that we arrived at the shoot-out phase. Carlos Alberto was a Rolls-Royce of a player and after joining us in July 1977 he transformed the team. His positional sense allowed Beckenbauer to play in more advanced positions. He always seemed effortless in his movement and was always in the right place at the right time. In this shoot-out against the Minnesota Kicks, Carlos flicked the ball forward so that it bounced on to his knee. He then stepped forward and volley-lobbed it over the advancing keeper to score. It was one of the most astounding pieces of skill, under extreme pressure, that I have ever seen. Carlos was a cool customer who liked his cigarettes, and you almost felt that he could have accomplished this skill while lighting a cigarette. When he was asked about his coolness under pressure Carlos replied, 'They pay me to be cool.' Carlos was a vital cog in our team; a superb player. Beckenbauer scored the winning shoot-out goal.

The rest of our progress was reasonably serene. For the second year in succession we found ourselves in the Soccer Bowl Final – this time against the Tampa Bay Rowdies. The 'white Pelé', Rodney Marsh, pulled out before the game. Chinaglia scored his 34th goal of the season and Dennis Tueart scored two, while I played my part with two assists and gained another Soccer Bowl title.

I did get to play one more game for Cosmos in 1978. A three-match exhibition series had been arranged to raise money for charity. The first game was against Chelsea at Stamford Bridge, and I was able to play before beginning my career at Coventry City. The presence of a new team-mate next to me in the changing room made me suspect another reason for these games. I later learned that Johan Cruyff had been persuaded to play three matches for Cosmos in the hope he would sign. I had no idea about this, and it was a thrill to find myself alongside the three-time European Player of the Year. I know it was only an exhibition, but we outplayed Chelsea that day and Cruyff was a major factor. He was still a superb player, and he, along with Pelé and Beckenbauer, could now tell the world that he had played with Steve Hunt.

Reflections – back at Cosmos in '82

I have no regrets about going to Cosmos. I improved as a player and played with the game's greats. America also provided a fund of stories to dine out on. Many of the established greats enjoyed the relative anonymity of life in America. Franz Beckenbauer, for example, was well and truly exhausted from over a decade of press attention in Germany. From a football sense many of these players had nothing to lose. If they were in decline they didn't have the pressure of the press and supporters in their own country saying they couldn't do it anymore. As Gordon Banks said, 'I didn't want people saying, "I remember when …"'

The politics at Cosmos are covered in *Once in a Lifetime*, and there is no doubt that Giorgio consciously set out to make himself influential. He cultivated his relationship with Steve Ross, and Gavin Newsham may be correct in speculating that Steve subconsciously wanted to be Chinaglia.

When I arrived at Cosmos, Gordon Bradley was the manager. He impressed me as a quietly spoken man with a good knowledge of the game. He was ably assisted by Joe Mallett, another quiet man who managed to convey a sense of authority. The problem for Gordon was that he had to create a team from disparate elements. It was like the United Nations – we were drawn from countries with differing football cultures, and although not a long-ball man, Gordon's tactical approach was based on an English style. I know that Gordon and Johan Cruyff fell out over tactics at Washington Diplomats. Typically, Joe, who was Gordon's assistant manager at Diplomats, acted as mediator.

The other problem for Gordon at Cosmos was Chinaglia. After I retired, I went to Virginia to coach some kids. I had just got married to my second wife, Kirsty, and was eager to show her New York before my coaching started. I had always had a good relationship with Gordon and Joe, and met up with them and their wives in New York. We chewed the fat about Cosmos and it was very evident that Gordon visibly bridled at the mention of Giorgio's name. Gavin Newsham, in the book *Once in a Lifetime*, tells a story about Chinaglia walking into Steve Ross's office at Warner Communications and helping himself to Chivas Regal from Ross's drinks cabinet. Apparently, Gordon told this story because he was in Ross's office at the time. Gordon didn't tell *me* that, but I can confirm, from that social meeting in New York, that Giorgio was not on his Christmas card list. Gordon held Giorgio responsible for undermining his authority at the club, and made it quite clear that he knew that Chinaglia was whispering in Ross's ear. The result was that Gordon was moved upstairs, and Eddie Firmani – Chinaglia's choice – was made the new coach.

I got on well with Eddie and know that he valued me as a player. He was constantly ringing me after the first season to persuade me to go back. He also made some terrific signings, particularly Bogie and Dennis Tueart. I was playing for Coventry when Firmani was sacked but I did hear that Chinaglia was also responsible for Eddie's downfall. When I went back in '82, I was told that Firmani had fallen foul of Giorgio after Eddie had substituted him in a game. I can assure you that Giorgio was not the type to meekly accept substitution.

I do know that Chinaglia is the best finisher I ever played with. Chinaglia liked playing with two wingers. It suited him because of his hunger for goals, but in a 6-0 victory over Toronto Metros I outscored him with a hat-trick to his two. The other goal was scored by Jomo Sono, a South African who was being touted as Pelé's replacement at the end of the season. Who could live with the pressure of replacing Pelé? On this occasion, however, he scored a goal even Pelé would have been proud of. It was one of those goals that seemed to defy science because the angle looked impossible.

One of the great characters at Cosmos was the full-back Bobby Smith. Bobby was a larger-than life character, and with his long hair and beard he reminded me of a grizzly bear. Bobby was a warm guy but he didn't take kindly to being left out of the side. One day Gordon Bradley told him he wasn't playing, and Bobby responded by obliterating the changing room. Bobby loved music and one evening invited me to see a band in his native New Jersey. I was unable to make it. It was only later that I discovered the band was Bruce Springsteen and the E Street Band.

The Cosmos player I was closest to was Gary Etherington. Gary was very supportive when Sue and I first arrived in New York, and was one of the good guys. We didn't have a car, and Gary was very generous in giving me lifts to training and helping us settle in. Gary was an excellent player who began as a winger, but he could play in most positions and do a good job. He won seven caps for the US national team.

Genius may be an overused word but Vladislav Bogićević (Bogie) was a football genius. Bogie came to Cosmos in 1978 from Red Star Belgrade. His left foot was a magic wand. Tall and with a straight back, he had the strength to hold opponents off, while manipulating the ball to make space for the killer pass that few players would even have seen. In a game against Seattle, Bogie scored with a header from my cross. My cross was named by WNEW broadcasters as the winner of the Getty Play of the Game Award. What pleased me the most was that Bogie characterised my cross as 'a magic ball'. For me, this is the equivalent of a young songwriter being told by Springsteen that he had written a great song.

One of the conditions of my transfer from Cosmos to Coventry was a game organised in New York between the clubs. I told my Coventry team-mates not to underestimate Cosmos. I didn't think they were ready for Bogie. As we came off at half-time, my Coventry colleague Andy Blair said, 'I just can't get near him.' Bogie had a habit of being sarcastic. He wasn't the kind of bloke who responded well to being told what he should do off the park. He once said of Firmani, 'He tells me how many cigarettes I smoke, how much beer I drink and what kind of shoes to wear.' Bogie was partial to a cigarette and a glass of beer. I regard him as one of the most gifted players I ever played with or against.

Some of the journeymen younger players, the early British imports, were driven by a sense of adventure in going to America. Many loved the lifestyle and stayed, enjoying the extra money on offer, and glad to escape a night on the subs' bench on a cold night in Barnsley. But Sue and I had missed home and had struggled with the change of culture. The homesickness had eased by the second year but the playing schedule and the travelling were murderous. For me away trips were the worst part of American football; you could often be away from home for five days. These journeys became more tolerable when the club paid for Sue to accompany me.

For a brief period in that second year I struggled with my game. In the first season I had been an unknown and the opposition didn't see me as the main threat. In that second season, I soon found myself double-marked, closed down and kicked. I can remember a game against Philadelphia Fury when I was booed aggressively by the crowd at Giants Stadium, and I made the mistake of gesturing offensively to the supporters. I received a ten-day suspension. I was struggling, and really appreciated the support of Bobby Smith, who pointed out to the press that I was only 21, and said the crowd should be patient. I was beginning to think about my game, and discussed the problem with Eddie Firmani. I would switch wings with Dennis Tueart. This allowed me to come inside, giving me more shooting opportunities with my left foot. Dennis was a superb, mobile, intelligent player. He was a huge help to me in that second season at Cosmos. The turning point for me was a game against Los Angeles Aztecs. At the beginning of the game I was booed, but by the end they were cheering me. I had a good game and scored the winner.

As I write this I have learned that Cosmos have been revived and are about to play in the US third tier. When I went back to Cosmos in 1982, Júlio Mazzei was the manager. To the best of my knowledge he is the only football manager in history who was a professor. I know they called Arsène Wenger 'The Professor' but he was only one in the same way that Doctors John and Hook were doctors. Yes reader, Wenger wasn't a professor, and Dr John, the great New Orleans pianist, wasn't a doctor.

Professor Mazzei was a real professor, but academic qualifications meant nothing to Bogie, who was his own sort of genius. When the Prof. asked him to run up and down the pitch in a 4-2-4 formation, it was a bit like asking Rembrandt to paint the outside of a house. I don't speak Serbian, but I think he shouted something like, 'Bollocks to this. Drop back into midfield, Steve.' I did, but I'm not sure Prof. Mazzei noticed the change to 4-3-3. I must say though that he was a charming man. He took the trouble to write to me after the 1982 play-off title victory, 'Dear Steve and family, I had no chance to say goodbye to you and your lovely family. It was an honour and a pleasure for me to work with you this season.' The Prof. didn't learn that courtesy at the Ron Saunders charm school.

I was 26 when I returned to Cosmos in 1982. I came back to New York with Sue, and by this time we had two children, Simon and Natalie. There had been an approach from Portland Timbers where Vic Crowe was coaching, but I was legally obliged to rejoin Cosmos if I went back to the NASL. The Cosmos team was still high quality. I had always associated Dutch players with Total Football: a cultured passing game and a high level of skill. Johan Neeskens, who was at Cosmos when I went back in 1982, had all these qualities, but he also brought a tough-tackling game with him. Neeskens was one of the few players who could effectively slide tackle on astroturf without burning his legs. When we played the equivalent of today's *rondo* style you quickly learned that you had to get rid quickly, or Neeskens would come clattering into you. Another hard man from Holland was Wim Rijsbergen, who is now the manager of the Solomon Islands. He was also at Cosmos when I returned in 1982, and was one of the toughest competitors I ever played with.

It was a thrill to return and be welcomed by Giorgio's comment that Dennis Tueart and I were the best two wingers he had ever played with. I made all three goals in my first game against Chicago Sting, and it felt good to be back. I was a much improved player. I was more composed on the ball, and was soon making and scoring goals. I was enjoying my football, and we had a beautiful home in New Jersey. This was a happy period in my career.

My goal against Tulsa in the 88th minute took us into the semi-finals of the NASL play-offs, which we won against Fort Lauderdale. The final was against our old foes, Seattle Sounders, who were now managed by Alan Hinton, the ex-Derby player. Mr Chinaglia, of course, scored the winner in what was Carlos Alberto's final game.

When we flew out for the Soccer Bowl Final in San Diego there was a private jet for players and cheerleaders, and a separate private jet for family and friends. Sue and the kids stayed in a hotel where their rooms were festooned with toys and presents – all courtesy of Warner Communications. In the hotel there was a room set aside with Atari products for the children to play. Sue and the kids were even taken out for a trip to San Diego Zoo. Steven Spielberg was the guest of honour at the party in our hotel after the win. At about 11pm, an announcement was made that the party was over and that the bus had arrived to take the families back to their hotel. I was thinking that this seemed a little early when another announcement came through, 'Now the party can really begin.'

Cosmos remained a good side that season, but it was clear that standards were in decline at some of the other clubs, and so were the crowds. Even at Giants Stadium the attendances were down to an average of 28,000. Some clubs were giving tickets away to make the numbers bigger.

The figure for the 1982 final was a paltry 22,634, and the writing was on the wall. Whether men's soccer will truly take off in America I don't know. It will be difficult to compete with American football and baseball. The lasting effect of the glorious Cosmos years can, however, be seen at grassroots level, and particularly in the women's game. When I see the all-conquering American women's team, I like to think that I played a small part in inspiring soccer mums to take their girls to play football. There has been a massive improvement in the women's game and I am pleased that a growing number of girls are playing in Britain. A friend told me about his mate's daughter, Molly, who grew up with pictures of the American women's team on her bedroom wall and was inspired to play. It is a beautiful game for both sexes, and although the NASL folded, soccer is now a permanent fixture in American grassroots sport.

The film, *Once in a Lifetime,* represents a Cosmos I only part recognise. In *Rock 'n' Roll Soccer,* Ian Plenderleith suggests that the Cosmos were characterised by Warner Communications as a party team, and that this was because Warner were in the entertainment business. Pelé and Beckenbauer may have found themselves in a number of nightclubs to gain publicity for Warner and Cosmos. I can tell you that it didn't affect their training or playing. They were true professionals. There was a divide between the superstars and the rest, but these two were elder statesmen and, in any case, that young/old divide tends to happen at most clubs.

My closest friend at Cosmos was Gary Etherington, and I tended to gravitate to the American players. They were closer to my age. Apart from the couple of spats I have described, the focus at Cosmos was on winning games. If, in my final spell at Villa, the players had shown half the commitment of Pelé and Beckenbauer, we may well have stayed up. Carlos Alberto was also a brilliant trainer; even in small-sided games he was intense. Playing with these players really improved my game and gave me a life-long commitment to work hard at my game. Playing for Cosmos strengthened my belief in the principles of possession football and playing out from the back.

In *No Hunger in Paradise*, his brilliant book largely about the academy system, Michael Calvin writes about a young man called Kieran Bywater. Kieran had been released by West Ham, having been in their academy for several years. Initially determined to make a career in the game, he was going from trial to trial, and was unhappy. He decided then that he wanted to recapture his childhood love of the game and have fun playing. To this end, Kieran moved to the US to play for the University of Charleston and do a four-year degree course at the same time. His motivation

'Use both feet Steve', but I knew my left foot would do most of the work.

'Could you think about giving me a testimonial in about 19 years Doug?' Villa boys meet Doug Ellis. I am second from the right at the front.

I was an apprentice at Villa when Santos played at Villa Park. Little did Pele know that the long-haired boy with the cheeky grin would be man of the match in the great man's final competitive game.

I am third from the right on the front, for some reason Ron Saunders saw fit to get rid of most of that successful youth team.

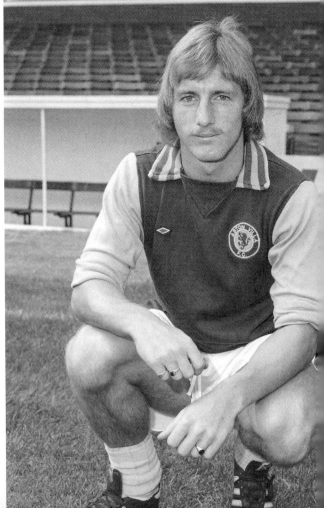

'Give us a game Ron.'

Home debut. Promotion secured. Sunderland guard of honour. Half a mile from Brantley Road.

With Joe Mallett after the '77 final – a lovely man.

Love love love Pele's farewell. He played one half for Santos and one half for Cosmos.

True ecstasy.

'Stop going on
about '66 Steve,
you were only
10'.

Frampton
comes alive.

'See you at Studio 54? I'm more a pub man Mick.'

With George Best. Flanking my football hero with my best pal at Cosmos, Gary Etherington.

Playing for Cosmos against Chelsea at Stamford Bridge. My only game with Johan Cruyff. Like Pele and Beckenbauer, he could now tell the world he had played with Steve Hunt.

'Everything is big in America.'

'You can't stick your fingers in your ears holding those, can you Steve!'

was to find happiness playing football and study in a very different environment.

Although, when I moved to Cosmos, I was still of course in the professional game, I can identify with Kieran's argument. It was quite obvious to me that Ron Saunders wasn't going to play me regularly, and as a consequence I may have ended up scrapping for a contract in the lower divisions. Although, as I have said, when I first moved to America I struggled for form, there was a sense of liberation in playing in that different environment. Yes, I was nervous about playing with Pelé, but I soon started to enjoy my football, and managed to recapture some of that child-like happiness in playing the game. I loved playing the type of game we played at Cosmos. I am often asked if I would have exchanged my Cosmos years for European Cup glory with the Villa. It is a hypothetical question because Ron wouldn't have played me, but my answer is 'no'. I would never have become the same player without those Cosmos years.

In 1982, the NASL had been reduced to 14 teams in a desperate attempt at economic viability. Even though you might think reducing the size of the league would have improved the quality, in effect the standard of the other sides was worse than I remembered from 1978. It was in 1982, my last season in America, that Phil Woosnam was ousted from his position as NASL commissioner. His statements had been perpetually optimistic, but fewer and fewer spectators were attending games. The idea that soccer could remotely rival the attractions of American football and baseball now seem totally fanciful.

By 1983, the NASL had nine clubs, and even Cosmos was no longer a viable financial proposition for Warner Communications. By 1985 Neeskens was the only star left at Cosmos and crowds were pitifully low. I say that the only star left at Cosmos was Neeskens, but that isn't strictly true, because the president of Cosmos in the club's dying days was a Mr Chinaglia. Fittingly, Cosmos played their last game against Lazio at Giants Stadium. The president of Lazio knew the president of Cosmos very well; in short, it was none other than Mr Chinaglia. Yes, Giorgio was president of both clubs. The crowd for that last game was 7,000. To place that in perspective, remember that 2,000 people had turned out to greet Chinaglia in the early hours at a railway station in Rome. In 1985 Chinaglia refused to pay the $250,000 performance bond to the league, and after he had threatened to throw the organisation's lawyer out of the window, Cosmos expired and so did the league.

Television is of course a major factor in the continued success of the Premier League in England and it is possible that the NASL would have survived with television money. I suspect, however, that not enough people in the States love soccer enough to watch it on TV. The real problem was that the clubs were losing a fortune. Even Warner decided that they could not afford to subsidise Cosmos when Atari, their computer game section, was losing masses of money. The fact was that, after the Cosmos' spending spree, every other club tried to copy them. They simply didn't have the resources: with fewer and fewer spectators, the NASL, and the clubs in it, were no longer viable.

In 2026 the US is staging the World Cup again. I hope that in the years between now and then the game takes off. Arsène Wenger suggests that the training of coaches is the key, and he also suggests creating centres of excellence where the best young players can train together. I agree with him. Whether excellent coaching will be enough to tempt young American men away from traditional American sports, however, remains to be seen.

4

You Want a Cathedral?
Coventry City Song

Led Zeppelin! What league are they in?

When I met Ahmet Ertegun in London and agreed to a second season at Cosmos, it had already been decided that I would have the option of joining Coventry City at the end of the US season. Nevertheless, when Gordon Milne and Ron Wylie came to check my form at Cosmos they had a wasted journey because I was suspended. They knew what I could contribute though, and the move was agreed with the proviso that a Coventry side, including me, would play Cosmos in New York.

Before my first match for Coventry, against Derby County, Bob Bryant wrote in the *Derby Evening Telegraph*, 'It needs a man of either undying ambition or gross insanity to reject a financial inducement that would give them security for life in a sport that disgorges men in their prime and spits them into obscurity. I am happy to report that Steve Hunt fits into the first category.' It is true that I turned down a lot of money to stay at Cosmos, and that I had the strongest urge to prove myself in English football. It is also true that I have never regretted my decision. My two England caps, and my consistent level of performance at home, is a legacy I am proud of. It is also true that Bryant was more accurate than he imagined because, as you will learn in a later chapter, I did feel – when I retired through injury at the age of 30 – that I was, almost overnight, thrust into obscurity. I do feel that this quote from Bryant raises the issue that in my day, many clubs failed to fulfil a duty of care to their players.

My first game for Coventry was against Tommy Docherty's Derby, and I couldn't have wished for a better start when scoring against a side with Roy McFarland, Colin Todd and David Nish at the back. In the early days at Coventry I played on the left wing; Tommy Hutchison was on the right. Gordon Milne was committed to attacking football, but the truth was that we were sometimes too naïve for our own good. A brilliant West Brom side with Laurie Cunningham, Cyrille Regis and Tony Brown slaughtered us 7-1. I was left out after that game. Gordon's commitment to attack, along with a 4-2-4 system, had left us very vulnerable. For a short while when I got back in the side I played on the right as an inverted winger, but I struggled for form. The system Gordon played felt rigid compared to Cosmos where Tueart and I switched wings quite naturally. A return to the left brought an instant improvement in form, and I particularly remember a game against Southampton in which I made goals for Ian Wallace, a brilliant predatory striker, who scored a hat-trick in a 4-0 win.

In May 1979 the game between Cosmos and Coventry took place. When we arrived in New York, we were taken to a restaurant at the top of the World Trade Center. I went up in the lift with Gordon Milne and Ron Wylie. I couldn't help taking pride in my welcome as players and staff came to the lift to greet me, 'Hi Stevie, welcome home! Great to see you.' I felt like a visiting hero. I'm not sure if Gordon and Ron wanted to take me down a peg or two, but when we were all invited to Studio 54 (a fleet of limousines had been ordered to take us there), Gordon put a stop to it by saying that we had a game to play. It was a friendly. I got on well with Gordon, but he made the wrong call. I think he was peeved about something, because that evening I was enjoying a beer in the hotel bar when I was told that if I carried on drinking I wouldn't be playing. I don't think that would have been a wise thing to do on Gordon's part, and I don't think that Gordon would have stopped me from playing, after all I was the reason why the team were there.

Gordon and Ron were a good team. Gordon was quite a reserved man who carried a quiet authority and was very fair. He liked to play with wingers. In attack it was an old-fashioned 4-2-4 with Mick Ferguson and Ian Wallace in the middle. Tommy Hutchison and I were out wide, but the system could leave us exposed, and Tommy and I had to tuck in when we were out of possession. This was a hard-working Coventry side with good team spirit, and it was generally a happy period in my career. Even so, the first few months were not easy. Although I scored on my debut, it took a while to get up to pace with the sheer physicality of English football. During this early period at Coventry, while struggling for form, I was dropped and selected for the reserves. Not to put too fine a point on it my performance in that reserve fixture was embarrassing; I was feeling sorry for myself and did not give my best for the team. If I had played badly and had given everything it was nothing to be ashamed of, but after that reserve fixture I felt ashamed. It never happened again.

My regret about the era in which I played was that the pitches were so poor. Maintaining possession was difficult on those muddy, uneven surfaces and the emphasis, even with a manager like Gordon who believed in good football, was on hitting the centre-forward early. I had always had the ability to whip accurate balls into the box with my left foot, and most goalscorers love the early ball. No matter how good you are at crossing you are always dependent on a striker making good runs. I can remember Gary Lineker saying he might make 20 runs in a game in anticipation of a cross. He said maybe he would only be on the end of one or two, but because he had made that early movement he had stolen a yard from that defender and a goal would often result.

Wallace and Ferguson were both excellent strikers and scored a lot of goals. They had thrived on playing with Hutchison over the years. Garth Crooks – who I played with later at West Brom – was a master at stealing a yard on a defender. As a coach, I always encouraged strikers to make their movement before the ball was struck.

John Beck, who was in that Coventry squad, was a very skilful footballer. It was a shock to me when he became a disciple of the long-ball game. I saw the Cambridge side he managed with Dion Dublin and Steve Claridge up front. John's gameplan was simply to hit the channels early, bypassing midfield to win second balls in dangerous positions. I guess they were playing to their strengths, but it was a tough watch. I was averse to long-ball football, although I could see that it could be effective up to a certain level.

I would have loved to have played on the surfaces that are standard for top clubs today. I also believe that as a hard-working winger and midfield player, I would have adapted to the pressing game that is so popular with the top teams in the modern game. Cosmos had broadened my football education, but I was lucky to find a club with a manager and a coach who had faith in me, and who were willing to give me a little time to adapt to English football. That Coventry side was a unit, and the team spirit was magnificent.

Physically, 1978/79 was tough. The Cosmos' season ran into the Coventry fixtures which meant 13 months of football. You might have thought that I would resist the temptation of a charity game, but when I heard Robert Plant was playing with me for Ron Wylie's team against a Gary Newbon XI I was very excited. I was a big Led Zeppelin fan. At half-time Ron said he was going to take 'that long-haired bloke' off. I told Ron that the 'long-haired bloke' was a hero of mine, and he agreed to keep him on. When Ron asked me who Plant played for and I answered 'Led Zeppelin', Ron's puzzled look suggested that he had never heard of Led Zeppelin, and I am convinced that he was thinking that Robert Plant was a winger from an obscure lower-division German side.

Jimmy Hill: And Ping

By the 1980/81 season I felt more at home in English football. I was beginning to see myself as a left-sided midfield player, and I think Gordon also saw that I could be effective in that role. I remained a good crosser of the ball and would still whip crosses in from the left, but I enjoyed the wider passing options from playing in midfield. In 1981/82 we had an even less experienced side. Ian Wallace had been sold in July to Nottingham Forest for £1.25m, money which helped fund the Sky Blue Connexion, the new training complex. Tommy Hutchison and Bobby McDonald were sold to Manchester City in the October. Looking back, it is clear that Hill's priorities were off the pitch, although Gordon Milne did manage to persuade Hill to invest in Gerry Daly who we bought for £300,000. Gerry was an experienced pro with a great football brain.

We were still a little naïve, but on our day we could be very effective. I enjoyed playing on the left with Brian Roberts, who replaced Bobby. He wasn't as creative as Bobby, but was a good tackler and always gave 100 per cent. Our partnership developed because we played together so often. There was very little chopping and changing in those days unless it was because a player had been sold, and, as Brian tells it, in *29 Minutes from Wembley* by Steve Phelps, 'This helped players develop their partnerships.' I had a similar relationship with Derek Statham at Albion, although he again was a very creative type of full-back; it is so important to get to know each other's game. I did notice when reading *29 Minutes* that Brian said we looked alike. Good-looking bloke, that Brian Roberts.

I hated playing in our awful second strip of brown shirts but I often had a good game when we wore them. A 3-1 win against Leicester, a game in which Gary Lineker scored his first league goal, is a good example. I was enjoying myself as a creative midfield player and I can't remember playing in a team in which there was such a good feeling in the group. Playing at Cosmos was wonderful, but as I have said, there was inevitably a divide between the established older stars and the aspiring younger players.

In some respects, Coventry could have been considered a club ahead of its time. While I was there the club purchased land at Ryton and built the Sky Blue Connexion, which included a training ground that was the envy of many big clubs. With squash courts and five-a-side pitches, it was a real community facility for a community-minded club. Unfortunately, we were also a selling club, and we were reminded of this in no uncertain terms when a Manchester City side containing Tommy Hutch and Bobby Mac beat us 3-0 at Maine Road. I read in *29 Minutes* that the Coventry side that day had an average age of 20; in that sense, the club was a cut-price version of the Borussia Dortmund of today – developing players to be sold to wealthier teams. Ian Wallace, who had been sold to Forest, came back to haunt us by scoring at Highfield Road in a 1-1 draw. We simply didn't have the experience to achieve consistency in the league. It is draining to fight with the spectre of relegation constantly haunting you, but fortunately a good League Cup run kept our spirits high.

It was fascinating in researching this book to discover the extent of Jimmy Hill's influence on the modern game. His contribution should be recognised by every professional footballer. In the simplest terms, Jimmy led footballers to liberty. When Jimmy was in his second term as chairman of the PFA, the maximum wage was £20 per week in the winter and £17 per week in the summer. For me, however, it was even more astonishing to find that when a player's contract ended, the club still held all the aces and could keep his registration and not pay him anything. In helping to abolish the maximum wage, and in establishing the freedom for players to move at the end of a contract, Jimmy deserves the respect of every footballer. I cannot deny that Jimmy deserves his place as an iconic figure in the game, and he proved himself to be an exceptional manager, leading Coventry to unprecedented heights in the 1960s, even hiring a Hungarian coach to introduce young players to the skills that the mighty Magyars had displayed in thrashing England.

A reading of Hill's autobiography will, however, quickly confirm that he was a man who found it difficult to reject the flattering advances of the great and good. His invitation to get involved in Saudi Arabian football is one such example, 'It was an appealing idea. Just to be invited to that enigmatic country, the centre of the Islamic world, was exciting. To be given the chance to advise them on my subject – even more so.' So it was that Hill formed an organisation called World Sports Academy (WSA) and sent out a team of managers, coaches and administrators who 'could inspire the Saudis to win the Gulf Cup'. Included in that team was the unlikely figure of David Icke, now a fellow Isle of Wight resident. I met David on the Isle of Wight when I coached his son, who was a decent keeper. Some familiar West Midlands figures in the WSA team included Ronny Allen and also Geoff Vowden, who had been so kind to me when I was injured in my first professional game at Villa.

The profits WSA made from what was ultimately an unsuccessful attempt to win the Gulf Cup were ploughed into Detroit Express in the NASL. Unfortunately, after a short while, the franchise was losing $1m a year. Hill's response, when the opportunity came, was to move it to Washington – partly on the back of an investment of

$500,000 from the Sky Blues. The result was another financial disaster, and Hill continued in his autobiography, 'With no other investment forthcoming, and WSA and Coventry City unwilling to provide further capital, the decision was taken to resign from the NASL.'

I can understand why Jimmy wanted to develop a world-class training facility and I can understand why he wanted an all-seater stadium; I can't, however, understand why Coventry frittered $500,000 on the Washington enterprise after Detroit had failed so spectacularly. Coventry needed investment. We had a very young side, and, to use Guardiola's phrase, we were 'running like bastards' to keep the club in the top flight. Hill himself tells us in his autobiography, 'We had to rely on our wits and rely on our youth policy to fulfil our aims.' He then goes on to tell us, 'The board came under fire for its stringent financial management.' 'Stringent financial management' does not seem to be consistent with a $500,000 investment in a doomed football club in America, and an argument could be made that the enormous sums spent on Ryton and on making Highfield Road an all-seater stadium would have been better invested in the team.

We had an excellent manager and a great bunch of young players, but we badly required experience. We had sold some of our best players and we needed a couple of top seasoned pros. Staying up in that 1981/82 season, with a spirited revival in the final months, is a memory that brings to mind the value of hard work and playing for your mates. When you hear a manager say, 'It is a good group,' it sounds vague, but I know exactly what is meant. That team was a good group.

There is no doubt that Jimmy Hill did a great deal for football and footballers, particularly in his work to abolish the maximum wage. He was a charming man who also did a great deal for Coventry City, but in looking back over these events, and in reading his autobiography, I can't help but feel that in his time as chairman he was too involved in enterprises unrelated to the club. Having a chairman who didn't attend Saturday matches sent the wrong message to supporters, and I am left with the conclusion that it was his own legacy, and not that of the Sky Blues, which took precedence at this time.

The highlight of that season was our League Cup run. The semi-final of that tournament still plays in my head. In *29 Minutes from Wembley*, Steve Phelps quotes the TV commentary of Hugh Johns after Garry Thompson's own goal had given us a 2-0 deficit, 'The night is beginning to turn into a total disaster for these kids from Coventry.' Garry was a terrific player and a good mate; I knew he would have been feeling very low. I cuffed him round the ear and told him to score at the other end. I was always up for the contest, but Highfield Road that night was electric and I was really fired up, so I turned to the crowd and clenched my fist as if to urge them not to give up on us. They didn't.

It is a cliché, but the crowd won that game for us. The spirit in that side was fantastic, and not one player would have thought of having a go at Garry, or Les Sealey, who had made the mistake that had gifted West Ham the first goal. Gordon and Ron were calmness personified at half-time, and the spirit in the dressing room, along with the atmosphere in the stadium, gave us a steely determination. Les was a very fine keeper and on several occasions that season he kept us in games. Garry, in scoring that own goal, had simply been tracking back and doing his job. He was a hard worker. I think we wanted to do it for Garry and Les, as well as for the crowd. Sure enough, in the 71st minute it was Garry who got us back in the game, and when Gerry Daly scored our second to equalise, the noise was unbelievable. With thanks to Steve Phelps, let Hugh Johns pick up the commentary after our winning goal, 'Well it's a dream come true for Garry Thompson. Three goals he scored tonight. One for West Ham and two for Coventry, and Coventry are in front for the first time tonight, 3-2.' Johns continued, 'It was Steve Hunt, the most improved midfielder in this Coventry side, to Garry Thompson and ping!'

Sealey's mistake for that first goal was untypical. He was a terrific keeper who I roomed with for several away games. He was a larger-than-life character – always talking, on and off the pitch. His career is largely remembered for his appearance for Manchester United in the 1990 FA Cup Final replay then the European Cup Winners' Cup Final victory over Barcelona a year later. He played brilliantly for us at Coventry. Les was such a vivid character. It was an enormous shock when he died from a heart attack, at the age of 43.

I used to compare Les to Arthur Daley. He was that type: always on the lookout to make a bob or two. He was also a good laugh and a lovely bloke. He had the footballer's instinct for daft, practical jokes, and I was the victim of one of them when, at a party at my house, I noticed that my Cosmos memorabilia, which I wasn't too shy to keep on display, had disappeared. I soon realised that Les was the guilty party and managed to retrieve my goods before they headed for the Bull Ring market. Les was a bit of an eccentric but he was totally dedicated to the game. He had been making a name for himself as a goalkeeping coach at West Ham – it was an awful loss for his wife and young family.

I have Les to thank for giving me the opportunity to meet the members of The Who. It was, again, another football connection. Les was a good friend of Alan Curbishley – the Blues midfielder – whose brother, Bill, managed The Who. Alan had managed to get me tickets for a gig, and Bill had helped arrange for us to meet the band backstage before the concert in Leicester. The members of the band were friendly and welcoming, but I had the sense that there was a certain tension between them. What I remember most is that Roger Daltrey was fretting about a mark on his white trousers, sending a member of the support staff to buy some Tipp-Ex to erase it. Somehow, it didn't seem all that appropriate for the voice of the nation's young, 'My Generation', to be worrying about a little stain on his trousers. This is the same guy who sang the great line, 'I hope I die before I get old.' Anyway, he seemed a nice bloke and it was great of Alan and Les to arrange that meeting.

I know that some people find it odd that the first leg of a two-legged contest, which we eventually lost, should be such a great memory. There is more to football than trophies. There was a unity and spirit in that young Coventry side which, on this occasion, was matched by the fervent atmosphere generated by the crowd, and we had a management and staff who all played their part as well. John Sillett, who was on the staff as youth team coach, and later won the FA Cup as manager of Coventry, was shouting instructions and encouraging us throughout the game. He was a wonderful motivator. Peter Bodak made a lot of goals for Coventry. He was a very skilful player, but John kept telling me to make sure Peter tracked back. Peter wasn't the best defensively, but everybody in that team worked their socks off that night. I know that we were all pleased for Garry and Les after what had happened in the first half of the game. Garry was one of the most underrated centre-forwards in the league. He was a really popular player in the dressing room, and I think that when he scored the winner that night we all shared his joy. That is the essence of team spirit.

Upton Park was an intimidating ground, and some of the lads thought the atmosphere was positively ugly for the second leg. This was a West Ham side with Brooking, Parkes, and Alan Devonshire, who was a brilliant player and very underrated. We were pleased to be drawing 0-0 at half-time and hadn't seen much of the ball but had defended with real determination, and even had a couple of good chances. On the hour mark, however, Paul Goddard scored for West Ham. The turning point in the game was David Cross's overhead kick to clear Garry Thompson's header off the line. Sometimes in football you get a feeling that it's not to be, and sure enough, Jimmy Neighbour scored their winner right at the death. Our youthfulness could on occasions work in our favour but, in this second leg, I think that experienced Hammers side simply had the experience to manage the game. It was actually one of the biggest disappointments of my career, but I think, like me, all the Coventry lads will remember that first leg as a microcosm of what was best about that Coventry side: young players working hard for each other and playing with determination. The first leg of that tie remains a precious memory.

Winning the ATV goal of the season award, for a goal against Birmingham, also stands out from that season. I picked up a loose ball near the centre circle and started to drive at the heart of the Birmingham defence. I saw Garry peel off and played a one-two with him, finishing with a curled shot, left foot of course, into the top corner.

When a manager shows faith in a player it gives that individual a strong incentive to repay his boss. I felt that about Gordon Milne. It probably took me a season and a half at Coventry to find my best form, and that coincided with a move to midfield. I suppose there is a balance between showing faith and not allowing complacency to settle. I can remember Ron Wylie telling me in no uncertain terms to 'get my finger out', or words to that effect. That set-to resulted in an open conversation about which position I felt best able to help the team. It was then that I was given the opportunity to play on the left side of midfield.

The arrival of Gerry Daly, and the emergence of Peter Bodak as a brilliant out-and-out winger, gave the side balance. Gerry was particularly thrilled when we beat his old club Manchester United, at Old Trafford, with a Hunt assist for Tommy English to score. Famously, Alan Hansen said you can't win anything with kids, but that young Coventry side with me, Daly and Andy Blair in midfield played with great spirit and no little skill. The problem, as so often with a young team, was that we could be inconsistent, but I am very proud of this period in my career and playing in that young team – so well-nurtured by Gordon and Ron.

Jimmy Hill became chairman in 1980, and displayed the silver tongue that made him such an effective TV presenter as he urged us to battle, in Churchillian tones, 'We will fight them in the mud' (or something like that!). I'm not sure it influenced the improvement in my form. I think Ron's short speech may have been more influential, but the move to midfield was the real key to my improvement.

Five points from the final three games took us to safety in 1980/81, but although we struggled at times, I felt it was a breakthrough season on a personal level. I had won the ATV and London Weekend goal of the season prizes, and topped the *Daily Star* First Division merit table. In other words, I had received the most points of any player in the First Division by the journalists of the *Daily Star*, who awarded points for every league game. I felt that I had at last established myself as a First Division player.

But by 1981/82 we were struggling again. Gordon and Ron carried the can and they were sacked. It was the usual story – spectators were staying away, and those who came were blaming management and players. The truth was that, although the club had invested in an all-seater stadium and under-pitch heating, there was very little investment in the team itself. Gordon had done an excellent job. Fortunately his successor was cut from similar cloth.

Watching Geese With Dave Sexton

Dave Sexton was similar to his predecessor. He wasn't a shouter, and he would generally make his points quietly. With Dave, you made sure you listened. He was ahead of his time and an astute tactician. There were, however, occasions when Dave made his points in an especially clear and simple manner. Before a game at Middlesbrough he came into the dressing room with a bottle of wine. It was not for drinking. On this occasion, Dave was a bit like Tommy Cooper with a prop. He hammered the bottle on the table several times, 'It's horrible here lads: it's cold, the pitch is terrible, the crowd will be at you and you're going to need this [bottle banged on table]. You're going to need a lot of bottle.'

Dave had a connection to the boxing world as his dad had been a boxer. He was a gentleman, but there was a hard side to him. At Coventry the training ground was near a car factory. We had just been beaten after a poor performance, and the factory workers gathered during their break to express their views. Dave didn't take kindly to their interventions so clambered halfway up the fence surrounding the training ground to confront them. The workers retreated. I think they could see that you didn't mess with Dave.

Dave had excellent man-management skills; he knew my son Simon was diabetic, and often asked me how he was getting on. I think most players appreciate this kind of interest and concern for staff and their families. It goes a long way. Simon's condition was diagnosed when he was three, and was a real source of anxiety. Simon had to be injected every day with insulin. They were tough times. It is not easy for a child to be told they can't have sweets and, to this day, Simon has to make sure that he eats carbohydrates every two hours. I knew that Gary Mabbutt was diabetic and in 1986, after a Villa v Spurs game, I asked him to have a word with Simon about the condition.

I cannot speak highly enough of Gary; he spoke at length to Simon who was then only seven or eight, reassuring him, and later sending more information and advice. From that day, Tottenham became Simon's second team after Villa. I am equally proud of all three of my children but in confronting diabetes from such a tender age, Simon deserves a lot of credit.

Young sportsmen with diabetes can learn from people like Gary. A current England rugby union international, Henry Slade, has diabetes. He wears a device to check his blood sugar levels so that he can inject accordingly. Simon has the same equipment. Henry, and the gadget that works so well for him should be an inspiration for young athletes with diabetes.

As I said, I had a lot of time for Dave Sexton, but he certainly had his eccentricities. I can remember when we were training one day and Dave suddenly shouted, 'Stop!' He started pointing at the sky. We looked up and saw a flock of geese flying overhead. 'They're off for the winter, lads. Right, let's get back to work.' I heard that Alex Ferguson used to talk about how Canada geese worked as a team when migrating. I think Dave must have been making the same point.

I made a transfer request in 1982. It didn't endear me to the supporters, and on reflection perhaps I made my views too public. I had been at Coventry for three and a half years and was desperate to win an England cap, but I had recently signed a new three-year contract and was in a weak position to demand a transfer. It was while I was warming up before a home game against Notts County that Jimmy Hill made an announcement over the tannoy, 'I want to inform our loyal supporters that it took our board only 20 seconds today to reject unanimously Steve Hunt's request for a transfer. He must honour his contract.'

After that game, which we lost 5-1, Jimmy came into the dressing room to air his grievances about our performance. Jimmy's displeasure did not alter the fact that the team needed experience. It was staring the board in the face. We could play badly and lose 5-1 to Notts County, but we could have good days and that season we reached the quarter-finals of the FA Cup. We had a brilliant manager, but I knew good form couldn't be sustained. I had heard rumours that Everton were interested, and selfishly, of course, saw this as a possible route to represent England in the 1982 World Cup. I concede that I made my request too public, but Jimmy's tannoy announcement was unnecessary. He clearly didn't want me to win the supporters' player of the year award.

As it happened, Sexton's excellent management, along with the commitment of that young side, eventually guided us to a respectable 14th in the table. I was in the preliminary group of 40 for the World Cup but was left out of the final squad, and at the end of that 1981/82 season I tried to numb my concerns that I would never win that England cap in the only way I knew – by playing football. I went back to Cosmos for the NASL season. Having spent the summer in America, I wasn't entirely sure if Dave would select me for the first game I was available for – against Everton. I note in my scrapbook that I am quoted as saying, 'I'm raring to go.'

I read an article recently about cognitive fatigue in sport, and the suggestion was that without adequate rest participants will suffer from exhaustion and make mistakes and bad decisions. I don't know about that, but I can tell you that at the beginning of the 1982/83 season I was knackered. I doubt that Dave would have selected me for that Everton game – I had only been back from America for a few days – if the squad had possessed more depth. In the previous match at Birmingham, Dave had been forced to play two 17-year-olds, Keith Thompson (brother of Garry), and Derek Hall. We happened to beat Everton 4-2, with Jim Melrose scoring a hat-trick; my cognitive fatigue couldn't have been too bad that day because I scored the other. I did though feel fatigued in some games. Between the beginning of the 1981/82 season and the end of the 1982/83 season I played 115 games.

I signed a new two-year contract, but even as I did so I remained concerned that the board wouldn't provide Dave with the resources to make us competitive. The crowds at Highfield Road were falling, and a Milk Cup defeat to Second Division Burnley, in front of the deserted terraces of Highfield Road, made me concerned about our prospects. In fact, our lowest attendance came when we won 2-0 against Brighton in front of a crowd of 8,054. Jimmy Hill criticised our performance against Burnley for a 'lack of effort'. I can assure the reader that no side of Sexton's lacked effort. We had a group of players prepared to do their best for the collective. We were not a side who could compete at the top of the table, but we played for each other and never lost sight of the collective aim.

On a personal note, I hadn't given up on representing England. I had represented an England XI against a London FA XI, assisting Kevin Keegan to a goal with a back-heel that Keegan himself described as 'a brilliant piece of improvisation'. I was encouraged when Keegan said after the game, 'Steve Hunt will definitely win an international cap and he deserves the chance.' Keegan was a player I greatly admired, and in my eyes he was a true superstar; a goalscorer, a brilliant header of the ball, and a man who played for 90 minutes with complete intensity. It was that intensity, as well as an underestimated natural ability, that really made him stand out.

It is said of tennis star Rafael Nadal that he plays the first point like the last, at full pelt. In an article by Stuart Fraser in *The Times*, on 6 October 2020, Stuart refers to an interview with Àlex Corretja, who twice won the French Open. Corretja was talking about knocking up with the 15-year-old Nadal. 'I played the first ball to him and his first forehand went boom. He hit it as hard as he could. I asked him, "How can you hit the first ball so hard?" Rafa's reply was, "I play at full speed from beginning to end."'

That sums up the furious energy with which Keegan played football. He was a leader of men, and if you didn't bring the same intensity to a game with Kevin Keegan in it, the odds were that you were in for a beating. The fact that Keegan had sung my praises gave me hope that, if I continued playing well for Coventry, the elusive first cap wasn't too far away. After Kevin had praised me, and I had represented an England XI, perhaps my head was getting too big because I can remember trying a nutmeg in Coventry training and suddenly finding myself on the deck after a couple of ferocious challenges from Steve Jacobs and Garry Thompson. They were telling me not to get too big for my boots.

Dave Sexton was a brilliant coach. I respected him as a man and a manager, but he had his hands tied; there was no money. Despite the signing of Gerry Francis, I could see nothing ahead but relegation struggles. Against the odds we did stay up in 1982/83 and I must give Dave full credit for that. Garry Thompson was sold to West Brom in February '83, behind Dave's back, but Dave retained his focus on the coaching. His excellent man-management and the sheer spirit of the side helped keep us up.

In his autobiography, Jimmy Hill complains that spectators were not coming to Highfield Road in the 1982/83 season, 'Even the visits of glamour sides did not fill the ground.' Oddly, he then pinpoints the reason for the absence of supporters, making the point that spectators are more likely to attend when their team is winning regularly. He argues that there wasn't enough money around, but a fortune had been spent on off-field ventures. Hill was right. Spectators want to see their team win. They would also prefer investment in the team to any number of fancy facilities. When Thompson was sold it was enormously frustrating for spectators as well as his team-mates.

I can remember Garry talking about the circumstances of his move to Albion. It is also documented in *29 Minutes*. The clear expectation in a phone call from Hill was that Garry was going to move. Ron Wylie was then at Albion and wanted him. Garry's wife was pregnant so he didn't want the upheaval. This didn't stop Jimmy attempting some emotional blackmail; he told Garry that the club would go bankrupt if he didn't agree to the move. While all this was going on, Sexton was being kept in the dark. I wonder how Hill the manager would have felt in Dave's circumstances. Garry had played 158 times for Coventry and scored 49 goals. Jimmy claims in his book that Garry was effectively superfluous because we had Mark Hateley. As Jimmy tells it, Mark had been playing on the left but wanted to play centre-forward. In football terms this was nonsense because, although Mark had been playing on the left, and would become a very fine centre-forward, he wasn't the finished article at this time. An ambitious club would have kept both.

Jimmy himself was under pressure as he had lost a great deal of money in America, but Coventry City had lost £500,000 on his ill-advised project in Detroit, twice the amount the club was getting for Garry. It was a mess. Furthermore, the man who kept us up despite this sea of troubles was sacked at the end of the season.

Jimmy praises Dave Sexton for keeping the team up, but it is faint praise. Here is Jimmy on Dave, 'He was yet another manager who, for better or worse, enabled Coventry to retain their treasured status at the top.' Curiously, he then goes on to criticise Dave for not being a 'tough entrepreneur'. Dave was a pure football man. He, and the Coventry players, performed a miracle in keeping the club up that season. In difficult circumstances he had nurtured some very talented players, like Danny Thomas and Mark Hateley. When those outstanding youngsters left, it became difficult to retain any optimism. Jimmy went, and the new chairman effectively reduced the wages of the playing staff. Of Sexton's team only me, Steve Jacobs, Brian Roberts and Gerry Daly were present at the beginning of the following season. I was looking for an escape route.

If Jimmy had wanted more spectators he should have invested more in the team. You didn't see a great deal of Jimmy at Highfield Road in those days, and he never attended Saturday games, presumably because of his broadcasting commitments. Nobody can take Hill's achievement as team manager of Coventry away from him; he also made an outstanding contribution to the game in many and various roles, but an absent chairman doesn't sit well with players or supporters.

I have mixed views on Doug Ellis, who made many bad decisions at Aston Villa, particularly in his managerial appointments, but nobody could deny the claret and blue blood in his veins. It is indisputable that Jimmy's affection for Coventry was genuine, but he had moved on in his business and media career, and the club was no longer his major concern.

I am as proud of those Coventry years under Gordon Milne and Dave Sexton as I am of any other part of my career. The players in those teams never stopped working for the cause. Many people may not think that survival is much of an achievement. For Coventry, in those days, it was. We stuck together. To be part of a team that sticks together in difficult circumstances is a wonderful feeling.

The Mask

I was unsettled at Coventry even before Bobby Gould came, but his arrival gave me an added incentive to leave. Some players respond to certain managers and not to others. I never got to know Bobby that well, but I had the impression he felt he could turn lower-league players into First Division players. He brought players in from the lower divisions and they initially provided energy and commitment, but the quality simply wasn't there.

Gould should, however, take a lot of credit for signing Stuart Pearce. Stuart was an inspiring presence on the pitch; his sheer will to win was a force of nature. In later years, when I was coaching at Leicester, I had a phone call from Stuart. He was coming back from injury and asked if he could train with my under-18 side. I jumped at the chance to give my young players a glimpse of a true professional. During that session Stuart worked harder than anybody. He played in training as he did in games: with total commitment. My young players left that session with a sense of awe.

Another signing Bobby made on loan was Charlie George. Charlie seemed a likeable character, but he was at the end of his career and wasn't fit enough to play at that level. He had been a very talented player, of course, but this seemed a strange signing. I know that my old coach Ron Wylie had signed him not long before for a club in Hong Kong. I don't know why he was released by Ron, but perhaps it should have sent alarm bells ringing for Bobby. Nevertheless, I was glad to have met him. He was a real character and a player I admired.

I felt that Bobby had some odd ideas. One day he hired some ballet dancers. Perhaps I am old-fashioned but I wasn't keen on prancing about in the gym, and I couldn't for the life of me see how it was meant to improve our performance. Gould may have had improving flexibility in mind, but to ask professional footballers to do pirouettes in front of TV cameras just seemed bloody stupid. I asked the manager if he was going to do it; the answer was no.

I took up karate when I was at Coventry in order to improve my flexibility; in fact I am convinced that karate reduced the number of injuries I received. Previously, I had been susceptible to muscle pulls and strains. I guess I was more a karate kid than a Nureyev, and I carried on with the karate long after I left Coventry. Talking of Nureyev, which I rarely am, I understand from *Rock 'n' Roll Soccer* that Franz Beckenbauer and Rudolf Nureyev lived in the same New York apartment block, and they occasionally hit the town together. According to Ian Plenderleith, Franz politely declined Rudy's advances. A Birmingham band called Locomotive had a hit with a song called 'Rudy's in Love'. Well I don't know if Rudy loved Franz, but, as you learned earlier in the book, my mum did.

I had been at Coventry for six years but I couldn't see how we were going to improve and I definitely didn't want to play long-ball football. Bobby had bought Dave Bamber, a 6ft 4in centre-forward, and the policy was to hit him early with direct play. It seemed to me that Bobby had been hired to build a side with bargains from the lower divisions.

There was no doubt that Bobby encouraged a strong work ethic, and in truth my state of mind may have been a little negative. I simply wasn't enjoying my football, and was fatigued by the previous relegation battles.

I know that Bobby later won the FA Cup with Wimbledon, but I didn't like his long-ball football, and I found some of his decisions very strange. One of Bobby's bright ideas was a match with the Coventry Supporters' Club. It seemed strange to risk the welfare of your players in such a game. I guess he thought it was good public relations. The outcome for me was a broken foot. The guy responsible was slow rather than malicious, but that's the risk inherent in this sort of game. I felt that Bobby and I were not a good match. I had felt in Dave's time that we were losing too many good players. Now I was really determined to move on.

In his iconic book *The Football Man*, Arthur Hopcraft writes about football management. He writes that Don Revie 'was determined that his own players would not be subjected to slights which he remembered in his day as a player'. Gould, in later years, said on radio that I was the most difficult player he had managed, but I felt this was more a reflection of our strained relationship. It may be a cliché but surely man-management and empathy are essential qualities for a football manager. In a game between Coventry and Southampton, the Saints player Steve Williams deliberately stamped on my hand while I was on the ground. I saw red and headbutted him, so quite rightly I was sent off. I knew I had been unprofessional. I was embarrassed by the incident and knew I had let down the team. Mr Gould had obviously not paid attention to Mr Revie's first law of football management, 'Do not slight your own players.' When I next reported for training I was forced to watch repeated playbacks of the Williams incident, with the entire Coventry staff in attendance – players, admin and auxiliary team members. I am not the sort of person who could forget this kind of treatment.

Shortly after the sending off, the Coventry team and management were staying in a hotel. I had purchased an old-man mask complete with long grey hair and an ugly face. I sneaked into Bobby Gould's room wearing the mask. I don't know how long I was there, but it seemed a long time. When he eventually came I jumped out of the bathroom and gave him the shock of his life. I promptly legged it down the corridor. To this day, I don't know if Bobby found out for certain whether I was the man in the mask. Bobby certainly didn't know on that day.

He appeared at the team meal in the evening with a face like thunder, demanding to know who had been in his room. I had been having a laugh with the lads about the incident; Bobby maybe picked up on this, and threatened a curfew on that evening if he didn't find out who it was. The footballers' code of honour remained resolute as they were a good bunch. We went without a drink that evening, but I had gained my revenge. Immature, I know, but he had annoyed me after that sending off. I knew I had made a mistake and I felt this was bad management on his part.

It is doubtful if a manager today could get away with embarrassing a player in this way in front of his staff.

It would be unfair if I failed to acknowledge that Bobby signed some of the players who won the FA Cup for Coventry in 1987, including Cyrille Regis. I was delighted, however, that it was John Sillett and George Curtis who led Coventry to glory. John had been sacked by Bobby, and returned to the club after Bobby was dismissed. George Curtis was a genuine hard man. He had a disconcerting habit of seizing your ears and biting your nose if he was displeased. Despite this, or maybe because of it, he was popular with the players who christened him 'Fred Flintstone'. It is worth saying that when John signed David Speedie after winning the cup he announced, 'Coventry City have shopped at Woolworths for too long, from now we are shopping at Harrods.' In four seasons under John, Coventry finished tenth, tenth, seventh and 12th. Highly respectable; I rest my case.

My career has come to be defined by the Cosmos years, but I remain very proud of my contribution to Coventry's survival and the club remains very dear to me. My best football was played under Johnny Giles at Albion, but generally I maintained a good level of performance which I felt should have gained me international recognition. In a struggling Coventry side I believe I gave everything to the cause, as did my team-mates. Fighting against relegation tests your resilience and confidence. As a 20-year-old, playing with Pelé, Beckenbauer and Chinaglia, I had to develop resilience and confidence. I also learned from their levels of motivation. I saw how hard they worked in training and matches. Maintaining motivation is a prerequisite for professional sportsmen, but sometimes a new challenge is required. I also wanted to play the style of football I believed in.

5

The Good, the Bad and the Baldy

I SUPPOSE my transfer to West Bromwich Albion might be described as a form of 'tapping up'. On Sundays I used to go to watch my uncle Dave's team, Brantley Rovers, play in the local park where there seemed to be at least 20 games going on at the same time. I was approached by Sid Lucas, the Albion chairman. I didn't know him but he introduced himself and said, 'Are you happy at Coventry, Steve? Do you think you might fancy a move?' Maybe Sid had heard that I wasn't enjoying my football. He was offering me a change I felt I needed. I met him at a hotel near the Albion ground and signed on the same day as Tony Grealish.

'Now Albion have the right blend,' wrote Gordon Cowans in his newspaper column. 'Grealish is sharp and positive in the tackle. Hunt is devastating when he goes forward.' We were a good combination. Tony was a holding midfield player who could also use the ball well.

Villa was my club, but I had a soft spot for the Hawthorns. From the tenth floor of the flat in Perry Barr I could see the three football stadiums: Villa Park, the Hawthorns and St Andrew's. As a kid I didn't venture much to the 'other side', south Birmingham, where the Blues were, but I did go to the Hawthorns. I would learn from watching the great players of the 1960s. I have already mentioned Bobby Charlton, George Best and Denis Law, but I can also remember seeing Alan Ball, Howard Kendall and Colin Harvey. I felt at home at the Hawthorns, and I felt at home playing with Tony Grealish.

My first home game was a 3-0 win against Stoke and it was my kind of football – a fluent passing game. With big Cyrille Regis up front there was end product. That match was also notable for a 38-pass movement. It was the type of football I had played at Cosmos. I enjoyed my years at Coventry and loved the club, but the last couple of years had been a struggle, and this was the style of football I wanted to play. Receiving a standing ovation from the Albion fans for the team's performance that day is a golden memory. I had scored my first goal for them, and I was named man of the match.

Although Albion had struggled in the previous season, this felt like the right move at the right time. I was 27 when I joined Albion and was determined to do well for the club and to put myself in the frame for England. Most important for me was the fact that I was enjoying my football. A win over Manchester United provided more evidence that I had made the right move. That result was our third victory in a row, and we had kept clean sheets in each of them. This was a United side containing Norman Whiteside, Bryan Robson, Ray Wilkins and Frank Stapleton, and I was playing as the passing midfielder I had always wanted to be. Steve Mackenzie and Cyrille Regis scored the goals in that victory. Tony Morley played on the left, and I think he appreciated my ability, having played in his position, to read his play. Our left flank was a great combination and I really enjoyed playing with Tony and Derek Statham, who was an outstanding full-back.

For a short period we had a formidable strike force of Regis and Garry Thompson, who I had played with at Coventry. They were both excellent footballers but they were also immensely powerful. I can remember a titanic battle at Tottenham when Cyrille and Garry were up against Graham Roberts and Paul Miller. It ended 1-0 to us, and I was very struck by the power of our strikers as they battled against two tough defenders. No quarter was given. Cyrille was the complete centre-forward – a great goalscorer and real team player. When I arrived at Albion, Cyrille remembered that when opposing him for Coventry

I tried to bring him down. I had simply bounced off him, and he said, 'You tried to do me, didn't you Steve? It didn't work, did it?' It didn't work. He was right. There weren't many who could stop Cyrille in full flight. I would have loved to have played with Cyrille for a longer period, but after eight games of my first season at Albion he was sold to Coventry.

I am not sure why Cyrille went, but I only know that I would have liked more minutes on the park with him. Like me, Cyrille played for Albion, Coventry and Villa (he trumped me by playing for Wolves as well). This short period at Albion was the only spell in which we played together. He left a huge impression. An incredibly strong, athletic player, he also had a great touch.

The Albion side that I joined provided the challenge that I needed. It was at Albion that I probably played the best football of my career. I had matured as a player and I tried to tell myself that the space between the white lines was my own space. This was where I could express myself. This feeling helped me to control any tension I felt. The best players monitor their own performances, and if I wasn't quite hitting the mark with longer balls, I would feel my way with shorter passes. I learned, as I got older, not to be too hard on myself. All top sportsmen have to evaluate honestly, but it can be unproductive to be overcritical. To be a top sportsman you need to have faith in your ability. There is a balance, a need to have faith in your ability, but it is also necessary to have the humility to know when you are not at your best.

Training sessions at Albion were like a breath of fresh air, and at the heart of those sessions were small-sided games played at high intensity. The emphasis was on quick, high-tempo passing played at match pace. There was no holding back. The people you wanted on your team were Johnny Giles and Norman Hunter, the assistant manager. When you played against them in training you knew that you would finish the session bruised and battered. The aim was to make the team match hard, but also to sharpen our passing.

I think Johnny could see that I could pick a pass. I had been educated at Cosmos, and there was no better teacher than Bogie. Playing in midfield for Johnny was a particular pleasure because he was one of the great passing midfield players. One of my proudest moments was after a game at Nottingham Forest. John came up to me and announced that I had given one of the best midfield performances he had seen for many years. I think that for that period at Albion, I sustained a higher level of performance for longer because I developed the ability to create pockets of time and space. Much of this was down to experience and learning. If you watch great footballers they often seem to be strolling when there is chaos around them. They don't panic, because they can see things early and can bring calm to the chaos. When I was in good form I sometimes felt that I had the ability to play at my own tempo – to slow the play down or to speed it up when necessary.

Bogie, at Cosmos, was a master at this. Gordon Cowans too. Perhaps the greatest example at a world-class level was Zinedine Zidane. I suppose it is about developing football intelligence. I have always felt that Wayne Rooney has a great football brain – an aspect of his play that in my view is much underrated. He had the ability to make consistently good decisions for the benefit of the team.

Paul Gascoigne was a wonderful player, but I sometimes felt that he was playing his own game, and would occasionally make bad decisions, sometimes holding on to the ball a little too long. His mastery of the ball was wonderful – he could pass long and short and was a brilliant ball carrier, but his temperament and nature sometimes got in the way of his decision-making. I was a spectator at the 1991 FA Cup Final when he made that awful challenge on Gary Charles. During the pre-match warm-up Gascoigne went in goal. In one way it was wonderful to see; a great player treating an FA Cup Final like a kick-about in the park, but he was clearly wound up. He lined up some footballs and aimed them at the hats of the marching military band. A bad decision, but not as bad as the one he made in assaulting Charles.

It is difficult to say how chemistry develops between players and managers. I learned a lot from Dave Sexton, and I can't understand why players wouldn't want to learn from such a deep thinker about the game. I regarded Alan Hudson as one of the best passers in the game, but I know that at Chelsea, he didn't get on with Dave. I have since read that Alan believes Guardiola is overrated, and that good players should simply be allowed to go out and play. Having read *Pep Confidential*, about Guardiola's first season at Bayern Munich, it strikes me that the most successful players want to learn. Alan was one of the best midfielders in the country, and I know that he found a soulmate in Stoke manager Tony Waddington, but I can't help but feel that if the world's best midfielder, Kevin De Bruyne, could improve under Guardiola, then players such as Hudson, a potential world-class player, would have benefited from listening to somebody like Sexton.

In *The Mavericks*, by Rob Steen, Dave Webb, Hudson's colleague at Chelsea, gives a clue as to why Sexton may have lost patience with Alan, 'He went way off the rails... He would never turn up for training on Monday morning...

He played the game to enjoy it all the time; that was his trouble.'

Alan played against us in my home debut for Albion against Stoke. He played deep and was still a wonderful passer, but commitment remains an essential ingredient for even the most gifted of players. There is nothing wrong with enjoying the game, but the very best players seem to enjoy improving. You do that by listening to the best coaches. You only have to watch Raheem Sterling to see how Guardiola can improve a player. I am sure the same applies to Klopp and other top managers.

There is an exchange to be made in professional football. You have to accept as a player that everybody at the club has a living to protect. The most fun I had in football was playing with my mate Dean as a kid in Perry Barr, or kicking about with my uncles in Brantley Road. For me, though, even in the professional game it was important to enjoy football. I tried to play with full commitment and still enjoy the game. The football we played at Albion was enjoyable, and even at the age of 27 I felt I was improving.

I said that I was enjoying my football, but I believe that today's game would have suited me better. The professional game in my era and before was marred by a certain brutality that isn't in the game today. The tackle from behind has gone and the game is better for it. When I hear punters say that it should be 'a man's game', I think, well tell me how you feel after someone has raked their studs down the back of your leg.

As a midfield player at Albion I had to develop a physical side to my game. I had to learn to put my foot in. On one occasion we played Wigan in a cup game. They had a tall midfield player called Kevin Langley who, as well as being a decent player, could be physical. At half-time, Giles and Hunter took me and Tony Grealish to one side. The instructions were to 'do him'. We did, and won, and I suppose that so-called 'professionalism' could spoil your pleasure in the sport.

It is a different game today, but it is a better one. In some ways, the skilful players of my generation and before deserve even more credit for finding a way to develop a platform for their skill. I always thought that John Robertson of Nottingham Forest was a wonderful player. It was uncanny how this slightly tubby-looking winger could turn defenders inside out. I was managing Willenhall Town when we played Grantham Town, where John was assistant manager to Martin O'Neill. I can remember being warmly welcomed by both men after the game. Real football men. I can imagine both men as players would thrive in today's game.

In my first season at Albion we were flying. It was a brilliant start to the season and we were playing good passing football. I knew that Johnny liked to play through midfield as I had seen a fair bit of the Vancouver Whitecaps, who he had managed when I was at Cosmos. It was my kind of football. We beat Forest 4-1 and John said that I didn't play a bad ball all game. He also said that he 'didn't think there was a better left-sided midfielder in the country' after that game. Unfortunately, one bad result can leave managers questioning their tactics, and the turning point came when we played Howard Wilkinson's Sheffield Wednesday, whose tactics were classic long-ball and we lost 4-0. I think Johnny Giles was badly affected by that defeat. He decided to mix our game up with a bit of long-ball stuff and I felt that was a mistake.

I think that bad defeats often cause knee-jerk reactions. We were playing well, and I didn't see why one defeat should result in a change of style. Often a bad defeat results in a manager being sacked, and I can understand how managers react to that sort of pressure. In my second spell at Villa, Graham Turner was sacked after a run of bad results including a 6-0 defeat. This only heralded the arrival of Billy McNeill and a disastrous season in which Villa were relegated (more of which later). In 2019/20, Southampton were beaten 9-0 by Leicester City. All credit to the Southampton board for keeping faith in the manager, Ralph Hasenhüttl. Southampton's directors were rewarded for that decision: they survived, played some excellent football, and are flying as I write this during the 2020/21 season.

Every football fan knows that Alex Ferguson's early years at Manchester United were not successful. The board kept faith and were rewarded with a full trophy cabinet. In *Pep Confidential*, it is clear that although he is not used to defeat, Guardiola is a manager who learns from his team's losses. In the quote that follows he is already thinking about Munich's forthcoming game against Real Madrid, 'Against Madrid, our two strikers need to tie up their entire back four; our wingers have to double up as full-backs, and in the midfield we need the best players who keep and move the ball for long spells of productive possession.' He then adds, 'We need to run like bastards.'

You may have gathered from reading this book that I prefer possession-based football. I understand that it is possible to win games with less possession than your opponents, but it is simply a personal preference. As I have said, the pitches in my era in England weren't the best, but another improvement to the game has coincided with the ban on tackling from behind. The best teams can now play football without having to worry about an opponent escaping punishment for a crude tackle. Although I enjoy watching good football, it doesn't mean that I don't appreciate the work that people like Neil Warnock, Tony Pulis and Graham Taylor have done. It seems to me that they all have the ability to foster good team spirit, and a framework in which the players are prepared to 'run like bastards'.

Sometimes managers are the right fit for a club at a certain time, but I have a feeling that at the top level the days of long-ball football are probably over. Yes, such tactics may keep teams in the Premier League, but the four best teams in the Championship in 2019/20 – Leeds United, West Bromwich Albion, Brentford and Fulham – also seemed to be the best footballing teams. I must give great credit to Sean Dyche for his work with Burnley as they play a direct game but they have remained competitive. I will be very interested to see how his career progresses. He seems to have fostered a brilliant team spirit, and I have a feeling that he will be capable of adapting to a bigger club and better players. To do that, however, he is going to have to change his tactics and style.

After the start we had made to 1984/85 it was a disappointment to finish in mid-table, but even the most pessimistic Albion supporter could not have anticipated the disastrous 1985/86 season. The departure of Garry Thompson to Sheffield Wednesday didn't help, but Johnny had signed two excellent strikers, Garth Crooks and Imre Varadi. Injuries to key players were damaging, but I am not convinced that Johnny's heart was in the job anymore. I had loved playing for Johnny, but I think he was beginning to think that there was more to life than football management. Of course the players must accept responsibility, but ultimately it is the manager who has to turn things round. Nine successive defeats told their own story. We were thrashed 5-1 by Manchester United in the penultimate game of that run, and the ninth defeat was 3-0 against Coventry. To his credit, Sid Lucas was highly reluctant to accept Johnny's resignation after the Coventry game, but I think John had decided that football management was no longer for him. It was a privilege to play for Johnny, who was a man of principle. Under his management I gained my England caps and played some of my best football. I owe him a great deal.

When Johnny left Albion he was replaced by Nobby Stiles, who had been working with the youth team. Nobby had, of course, been an old-fashioned enforcer. It has often been remarked that he was extremely short-sighted, in the literal sense, and I have never seen such thick glasses as the ones he wore. I know Nobby said that when playing Portugal in the World Cup, he could see three Eusebios, and that he would tackle the middle one. I'm not sure that he would have been a Guardiola-type player but he helped

England win the World Cup, and it is an absolute disgrace that he had to sell his caps and memorabilia. I know that it was tough for Nobby commuting from Manchester to Birmingham, but despite a couple of wins the results remained poor in this period. With two-thirds of the season gone we were 12 points from safety.

Carlton Palmer also played for Albion during this period. He had a long stride and total commitment. Like many people, I never saw him as a future international, but you couldn't fault his work rate. He was selected for England by Graham Taylor, and I would say that he was a Taylor-type of player. I don't know if Carlton remembers, but there was one occasion when he was asked to play at centre-half in a friendly, against what I think was a South Korean team. Carlton was a bit nervous so we told him to concentrate on marking their number nine. I know this doesn't sound very politically correct, but we informed him that their number nine was called 'Bang One In'. Once we got out on the pitch, Carlton asked, 'Where's Bang One In?' It was hard to stifle our laughter as we told him Bang had number nine on his back. Carlton got everything he could out of his ability, and it is a credit to him that he became an international. A great pro and a good bloke.

Nobby was replaced by Ron Saunders. I knew when he arrived that my time at Albion was coming to an end. As

I say, some managers are the right fit for some players and for some clubs. Ron is still held in high esteem at Villa, despite having also managed Birmingham and West Brom. He built the European Cup-winning side and I know that those players thought very highly of him. He brought them glory. Ron, however, wasn't the right fit for Albion, and he certainly wasn't the right fit for me. The problem for me was that Ron didn't fancy me as a midfield player. I had moved to midfield but I knew he wouldn't play me there.

It was reported in the *Argus* that I had 'battled, almost alone, to keep Albion up' in 1985/86. I don't know about 'alone', but I had played well and later was named player of the season. This seemed to mean nothing to Ron. It was a source of great frustration when Ron arrived and I simply don't know what he had against me. Almost my first conversation with him at Albion was on the team bus, when he said, 'Hey, baldy, come and sit by me.' Ron and I were never going to be mates. I had an idea that we weren't going to talk about our favourite films. 'I'm not going to play you in midfield,' he said. I had just had a good season individually playing in midfield. I had also become an international player. Ron then went on to say that he didn't want ball players in midfield. A curious thing to say, given that at the heart of his Villa team was Gordon Cowans – one of the most cultured players ever to wear a Villa shirt.

I didn't want to leave Albion, but I wanted to leave Ron so his presence at Albion made it an easy decision when Villa came in for me. Ron couldn't stop the rot, and it would be 16 years before Albion returned to the top tier.

My son Simon wanted me to stay at Albion. It was the only team he could remember me playing for and when I told him that I was going to Villa he stomped off to bed then wouldn't speak to me until lunchtime the next day. He is now a fanatical Villa supporter. The highest salary I earned was at Villa, in my second spell at the club. It was in the region of £30,000 a year, which was a good sum in those days but hardly enough to set you up for life. Young people, when I tell them I played football for a living, are always astonished that I don't drive a Bentley, and that I still have to work.

Last year I was invited back to Albion to receive a club cap, awarded to every living player who has represented the club. They looked after me and my family very well. As we approached the ground, I couldn't help but notice the players' luxury cars. I don't begrudge the players of today the money they earn, but more and more clubs are going to go to the wall if they continue to pay these salaries. It simply isn't sustainable at Championship level and below. I don't blame the players, however. I feel that the people who offer to pay unaffordable wages are to blame.

When I was growing up, three Villa players lived on Brantley Road. Of course, players deserve to be paid well – it is a short career, but as salaries have soared the connection between supporters and players has been broken. That is a pity. I was now going back to a club with which I had deep connections. I was glad to be leaving Ron Saunders behind, but I had been happy at Albion and was sorry to leave. I did, however, relish the idea of settling my unfinished business at Villa.

I returned to Villa Park as an England international having won two caps, both as a substitute. Johnny Giles told me in training that I had been selected for the squad to play Scotland and Russia. I was excited, but there are many players included in squads only to not make it on to the pitch. Bobby Robson, who chose me, was famous for not remembering names. When he first met me he called me Roger, presumably confusing me with Roger Hunt, the England World Cup striker. I tried to remain optimistic about gaining my first cap. My room-mate at the squad hotel in Troon was Gary Lineker, who was also uncapped, but he, unlike me, had time on his side. For me it felt like now or never.

6

Tackle Him! Bring Him Down!

I HAVE strong memories of travelling from Troon to Hampden on 26 May 1984. The closer we came to Hampden the more hostile the reception became. I knew the Scots were passionate, but this seemed like raw hatred. I tried not to make eye contact with any individuals lining the route. Let's just say I have rarely encountered such emotion before a game. From the pitch, before the kick-off, there seemed to be a continuous wall of tartan reaching to the top of the stands. To my eye the England fan representation looked very small as I sat nervously on the bench.

At half-time Bobby Robson took Mickey Hazard, who was also a substitute, to one side. I assumed he was preparing to bring Mickey on, and I was concerned that I might not win that longed-for cap. It was a surprise then, when the manager asked Gary Lineker and me to warm up. That was the most nerve-shredding time, warming up in front of those Scottish fans as I tried to control my emotions. Mickey never did win that first cap, a travesty in my view, since he was a skilful, cultured player.

When I came on for Mark Chamberlain and crossed that white line, I was focused on the game. I felt that I did reasonably well in the short time I had, making some decent crosses. The pace was unbelievably fast, much like a local derby, and I remember dwelling on the ball a little too long and thinking that I mustn't do that again. I think I did okay and it was a great privilege to play alongside Bryan Robson and Ray Wilkins. Bryan was a superb box-to-box midfielder, and a scorer of many important goals; Ray was a highly cultured player, elegant, and a wonderful passer of the ball. The minutes on the park went very quickly and the game finished 1-1.

Having won my first England cap, I wanted to let it all sink in and found it hard to leave the pitch. My thoughts at the end of the game were with my family. I went back to Brantley Road in my mind; to my uncles, and of course to my mum, who had stormed Vic Crowe's office all those years ago. My thoughts also went to Sue and my children. The FA awarded two shirts for internationals, and I was not going to swap one of them with an opposing player; one was for my mum, the other for my kids.

The following week I earned my second cap. You wait ages for a bus and then two come along. I had never played at Wembley and when I came on for John Barnes it was the fulfilment of another ambition. Representing England at the home of English football was a dream I had nurtured since early childhood. Unfortunately the game was less memorable, at least from an English point of view, as the team played poorly, and were 2-0 down by the time I came on. We were playing a very good Russian team led by their outstanding centre-forward, Oleg Blokhin. As with the Scotland game, I felt I acquitted myself well in difficult circumstances, seeing quite a bit of the ball and getting through quite a lot of solid defensive work against a Russian side which kept the ball well. It wasn't a good atmosphere at the end of the game. Many fans were disgruntled, and made their feelings known. Nothing, however, could lessen my pride at playing for my country twice in one week. Again my thoughts turned to the back garden of my nan's house in Brantley Road where it all started.

I read in a newspaper about Alan Jones who was awarded his international cricket cap at the age of 81. He made one England appearance against a Rest of the World XI. The ICC decided to withdraw Test status from that game, so Alan didn't win his cap, but in 2020 the ECB decided he should receive one. The picture in the paper of

Alan's big smile holding his cap shows his delight, and is equivalent to the joy I felt on winning my caps. I only made two England appearances, and maybe spent 40 minutes representing my country, but nothing can diminish the pride I feel in having done so.

I was disappointed not to get on the pitch again for England after the Russia game. I was chosen to tour South America but was frustrated not to get any minutes. England played three games, beating Brazil, losing to Uruguay and drawing against Chile. There was a big divide in the squad on that tour. Bobby Robson took 20 players but only used 13 of them. I thought I might be 'scuppered' when John Barnes scored his memorable individual goal against Brazil. The Englishman in me was thrilled to see such a brilliant goal, but as a direct rival for his position in the team, my head was in my hands as I wondered if I would get any game time.

Mike Brearley, the ex-England cricket captain, tells a story, in his book *On Form*, about an Essex batsman called Dickie Dodds who was out for a duck on a flat batting strip. By lunch the team had scored 150 without further loss, and the batsmen had made batting look easy. Dodds had the agonising experience of watching the batsman who had replaced him scoring runs which Dickie regarded as stolen property. As the not out batsmen came in for lunch,

Dickie confessed to one of them, his captain Douglas Insole, that he was 'full of bitterness' and not 'wishing you well'. I confess here to similar emotions as Barnes went on his amazing run, cheering him on from the bench but simultaneously I was inwardly urging defenders to tackle him or bring him down. It is human nature. I felt envious of Barnes every time he walked out for England, particularly if he retained his place after a poor performance. There was nothing personal in it, he was a wonderful player but envy plays its part in sport as in every other walk of life.

I still thought, however, that there might be the chance of some game time. The fact that all these games were friendly matches gave me some hope that Robson might give the fringe players some minutes. The magnificent seven, as I christened the fringe players who didn't get any action, were to be disappointed. I had at least already won two caps. Simon Stainrod, a fine player, had not been capped. Simon was not a shrinking violet and made his frustrations very clear to Robson. He never did get that cap.

I have been thinking of sportsmen who are often falsely described as nearly men. The golfer Colin Montgomerie is sometimes described as such because he never won a major. I have looked back at his stats; Colin won eight European Order of Merit titles and 31 European Tour events. He was second in the PGA Championship in 1995 and second in the Open Championship in 2005. In the US Open he finished second in 1994, 1997 and 2006. He finished third in the same championship in 1992. He is also regarded as one of the greatest Ryder Cup players of all time. Nearly man? I disagree. This level of consistent performance is what football managers dream of. Here is a list of one-time major winners: Ian Baker-Finch; Todd Hamilton; Wayne Grady; Mark Brooks. All of these players were no doubt fine golfers, but a brief look at their records, and a discussion with people who know golf, indicates that Monty, despite never winning a major, was a greater player and a true great. Consistency in performance is much underrated in sport.

You will no doubt have read this book and taken that I was driven to be capped for England. Yes, it was a constant driving force in my career; just as for Monty winning a major was no doubt a driving force. It is easy for me to say, because I did eventually play for England, but, can anyone argue that Dennis Mortimer, Howard Kendall, Mickey Hazard, Jimmy Case, Jimmy Greenhoff and Steve Bruce were not great players, in spite of not winning an England cap between them? In my view, Simon Stainrod deserved his chance on that tour of South America, and his frustration was understandable. Thinking back to my first cap against Scotland, as I have said, it could easily have been Mickey Hazard who came on. In a roundabout way the point I am making is that as I look back on my career, it is the consistency of my performances that gives me most satisfaction. I have been watching *All or Nothing*, the documentary about Tottenham, in which José Mourinho speaks to Dele Alli in his office effectively telling him that great players maintain consistency in their performances. I saw at first-hand how Pelé, Franz Beckenbauer, Carlos Alberto and Giorgio Chinaglia maintained a constantly high level of performance in play and in training. I never forgot that.

It wasn't just the fact that I didn't get any game time on that tour. The magnificent seven were made to feel like a fringe group; training separately and receiving very little attention from the coaching staff. I remember Don Howe taking the first team while Robson watched Clive Allen practise his shooting. In the meantime, the fringe group were 100 yards away, unsupervised, simply playing small-sided games. There was a big divide and it bred some resentment. It was a privilege to travel to South America as part of the squad, but our group all felt like outsiders and felt as though we had been badly managed.

In the final match of the tour, a truly awful encounter against Chile, Sammy Lee was brought on as a substitute. No disrespect to Sammy, who was a committed, energetic and good player, but Robson knew what he could give the side. Why not try Simon Stainrod? It would at least have protected Robson from Simon's anger at the end of the tour. I had been looking forward to working with Don Howe. He had a reputation as a brilliant coach. I didn't see any of that.

What surprised me most on the South American tour was finding out that some top international players appeared to be addicted to alcohol. I did drink when I was playing, and I still do like a drink, but there were some very heavy drinkers in that squad. I can remember one occasion on that tour which was a total piss-up. I was familiar with the drinking culture in English football, but I was genuinely shocked at the state some players got into. I have a great deal of sympathy for anybody suffering from an addiction. My concern is that there has been very little support for players suffering from those problems. It has taken an individual like Tony Adams to bring this matter to public prominence. I am sure that drinking is less of an issue at top clubs now but it is certain that, with their massive wealth, some modern players will be vulnerable.

While in South America I made my first excursion into the world of 'journalism', talking to Martin Swain of the *Birmingham Evening Mail*. I have got the articles in a scrapbook and note that I wrote about 'a brilliant individual goal by John Barnes against Brazil'. I think I must have spoken to Martin through gritted teeth. In fact, much as I admired Barnes's goal, there was a voice in my head saying, 'Tackle him! Tackle him! Bring him down!' It is not in a footballer's nature to want a player he is competing with for a place in the side to do well.

As I look back at the article, I note that authenticity is not the strongest part of my brief career in journalism. There was a part of me that was, like Simon Stainrod, thinking, 'Why have you brought me halfway across the world to sit on the bench?' I couldn't tell the readers of the *Birmingham Mail* what I thought, but I have no idea why I said the Chile game brought an impressive end to our trip to South America. It was an awful game and an awful performance; I simply didn't understand why Bobby didn't give the fringe players a run. Bobby is an idol on Tyneside and in Ipswich. His achievements speak for themselves, but his man-management on that tour left a lot to be desired. Don't just take my word for it. Ask any of the seven players who not only didn't get so much as a minute on the park and were made to feel like outsiders.

Kevin Keegan also had his doubts about Bobby's man-management, having learned via the press that he was to be left out for his first match as England manager. As Keegan points out in *My Life in Football*, 'It seemed incredible that Bobby never considered it the decent thing to pick up the telephone to explain.' Kevin had won 63 caps and was England captain. He never played for England again, and Bobby never spoke to him about it. In his autobiography Bobby acknowledges that he made a mistake in not contacting Kevin, yet it is mystifying that such an experienced manager did not consider phoning him. I have a great deal of respect for Bobby, and all he achieved in the game, yet it was so disappointing to feel like an outcast on the South American tour. A few words from Bobby, or Don Howe, would have worked wonders for the morale of the fringe players. Although I was proud to be selected for the tour, it felt that we had travelled halfway around the world for a little kick-about.

I was to sit on the bench twice more for England: once against East Germany, and finally for an 8-0 victory over Turkey. It is frustrating to see your team struggle without getting on to the park yourself, but equally in a one-sided game against Turkey you might have thought it was the perfect opportunity to try a few players. Some players kept their places despite performing poorly. John Barnes was a wonderful footballer, particularly in his Liverpool years, but that goal against Brazil raised expectations which ultimately he did not live up to for England. I think the system was too rigid for John at international level. He was at his best when given a bit of freedom.

An Impossible Job, the film about Graham Taylor's last games in charge, includes several people I came across in my football career. Firstly, of course, there is Taylor himself. During the clips of games throughout the programme, there is ample evidence that even with international players Taylor was fixated with the long ball. He had Gascoigne in midfield, but still appeared to want balls knocked into the channels. There is a moment when the camera focuses on a bemused Nigel Clough sitting on the bench. Perhaps he was bemused by the crude stuff the England team was playing, and was reflecting on what his dad Brian would have made of the job. In the film, Taylor comes across as a genuine person. Footage of him talking to prisoners during the programme is a measure of a man who took his wider responsibilities seriously. He did a wonderful job at Watford and Villa. England manager? He should never have been appointed.

I felt sorry, however, for the likeable Taylor as I watched him cross-examined by the blazered fools at the FA, having to explain why England had been beaten by some very modest teams, including the USA. During that meeting, up piped Charles Hughes, whose refined accent would make the Prince of Wales seem like a cockney geezer. Hughes really was an unlikely character to be proclaiming about the future of coaching. I find it quite bizarre that

Hughes was at the FA for 30 years. If you want to know why Taylor was appointed, and why Brian Clough never had a look-in, cast your eyes around the people in that room. They didn't have a clue. In one sense, Hughes was right – there should have been a blueprint for coaching. Unfortunately, Hughes did develop a blueprint, and it was based on the long-ball philosophy outlined in his book, *The Winning Formula*.

The flaws in our coaching system are reflected by the career of Joe Hart. A brilliant shot-stopper, it seemed that Hart was the future. He won 75 caps for England, but we found out when Guardiola released him that Hart was in fact the past. It just took a long time for the people running the English game to realise it.

When Guardiola arrived at Manchester City his first decision was that Hart was not good enough with his feet to play as a goalkeeper/sweeper in his system. Hart's career has been in decline ever since. He was an excellent keeper, but even in a side like Burnley, where it is not a high priority for the keeper to be good on the ball, he was unable to claim a first-team place. Clearly, his confidence was undermined by his rejection at City, so that even his great asset as a shot-stopper was suffering. In 2020 he was transferred to Tottenham Hotspur and I would like to think that at Spurs he can find the stability to restore his reputation as a brilliant shot-stopper. There are many questions arising from Hart's career. The first is why he was unable to develop the skills to find a place in Guardiola's side. Was he simply not good enough with his feet, or was he the victim of a coaching system that was too dogmatic to recognise that, especially after the change in the back-pass law, goalkeepers had to be excellent passers?

In *Zonal Marking*, Michael Cox points out that, in the early 1970s, Johan Cruyff was trying to persuade Rinus Michels that the Dutch team needed a goalkeeper who was good with his feet. Watching Manuel Neuer sweeping behind the high line of the Bayern Munich defence when they won the Champions League Final in 2020, it is hard to imagine how this aspect of goalkeeping was neglected for so long in this country. Alex Ferguson, in his book *Leading*, writes about how great footballers can only become great because they spend hours with the ball at their feet as kids. It is to be hoped now that kids who are good with their feet are given the opportunity to play as keepers.

Goalkeepers should no longer be regarded as a separate part of the team; it is essential in the modern game that they are comfortable playing as sweepers, but also that they have a range of passing enabling them to play accurate balls that can beat the first wave of a high press. Alisson and Ederson are both outstanding goalkeepers, and also brilliant passers. The current England number one, Jordan Pickford, is good with his feet, but in recent times his form as a stopper has been erratic. Nick Pope would be favoured to replace him if we were looking at stopper ability, but the general consensus at the moment is that he is not good enough with his feet. Pope is 28, and Hart has 75 England caps, the last earned in 2017. It cannot be disputed that these two keepers have been top notch as shot stoppers, but it is no longer realistic to select keepers at the highest level who are not good enough with their feet.

The problem was in the coaching system, in the fact that Charles Hughes persisted with a long-ball philosophy long after Cruyff was encouraging Michels to choose goalkeepers who could play with their feet. It is also the case that goalkeeping coaches had been brought up in an era when keepers were ranked according to their ability to save shots. I played against Shilton and Banks, two of the greatest in football history. Would Shilton and Banks get a game with Guardiola or Klopp? The answer is no. Why have we allowed two outstanding keepers, in Pope and Hart, to come so far without developing the technique to play football with their feet? The back-pass law was changed in 1992, the year Nick Pope was born. Pope has never seen a keeper pick the ball up after a pass back from one of his team-mates.

Hughes's *Winning Formula* was first published in 1990 – 16 years after Cruyff was persuading Michels to play a footballing goalkeeper. The section on goalkeeping has two paragraphs on what Hughes calls 'fly kicking', and one page on kicking from hand. Here is Hughes on fly kicking, 'If the keeper has to come out of his area to defend the space behind his defenders, he should concentrate on kicking the ball as high and wide and as far as possible.' There is not one word that encourages goalkeepers to be comfortable on the ball. It is true that the book was published before the back-pass law was changed, but that is no excuse for the shocking failure of vision. It is interesting to note that Cox refers to the fact that Cruyff, as long ago as the 1970s, believed the goalkeeper should act as an 11th outfielder, starting attacking moves and sweeping behind an advanced defensive line.

What Svengali-like hold did Hughes have over the FA? Why, at a time when Liverpool were the best side in Europe, and playing passing football, was Hughes in charge of coaching in this country? As recently as 2002, a friend took a coaching course with the Hampshire FA to find that the main point of reference was Hughes. This was a course designed to coach people to teach youngsters. It is clear that at last we are beginning to develop technical players who can keep the ball, but again there are simply not enough defenders, let alone goalkeepers, with the skill required to make the England team truly competitive at the highest level.

When I was at Cosmos, three players for each team had to be American. There are too few English players coming through with extensive first-team experience. Phil Foden may be the jewel in the crown, but we must let players of this quality gain more experience at senior level. It is true that Foden is learning from great players in training, but at the age of 20 I was playing week in and week out with Pelé and Beckenbauer. Game time is essential. Perhaps it is time to insist that a certain number of players in Premier League sides are English.

Hughes tells us in *The Winning Formula* that he had no disagreements with Charles Reep on the strategic philosophy he came up with. In fact, it was because it was the same strategic philosophy which was based largely on the analysis of games during the 1960s. I came across Hughes only once, and there is nothing personal here. I know he is still alive, and in his 90s, and I don't wish to upset an elderly gentleman, but the legacy of the Hughes philosophy has been disastrous for the English game. He didn't seem to be a football man.

I am not of the school that believes you must have played the game at a high level to be a successful coach.

There are plenty of Jose Mourinhos and Arsène Wengers who give the lie to that theory. Mourinho and Wenger strike me as football men who were open to different ideas. In *Zonal Marking*, Cox discusses the Italian coaching system based at Coverciano, the technical headquarters of the Italian Football Federation. The most famous graduate from that school was Marcello Lippi, 'That's what I truly found important about Coverciano – the exchange of ideas between myself and my colleagues,' Cox wrote. At its worst *The Winning Formula* is incredibly dogmatic, Hughes continuing, 'Direct play is the best strategy. All of the facts point to the conclusion that when the number of passes in a move exceeds five the chances of creating a scoring opportunity at the end of the move decrease.'

This is the inflexible nonsense of a man who hasn't listened to people who played Liverpool in the 1980s: play against the side which keeps possession, and you get tired chasing them. It is that possession play that causes fatigue in the opposition. Ultimately that fatigue leads to the concession of scoring opportunities. There is also the little matter of football as a spectator sport. Arsène Wenger once made reference to the spectator who, on going to a game, thinks that he might have a fantastic experience. In other words he is looking forward to seeing good football.

Sadly, as I write this, Jackie Charlton has just died. The tributes from his old Republic of Ireland players are heartwarming. I have just read a tribute article from Kevin Sheedy. He made a comment about the team's tactics, 'Over a period of time we took fewer and fewer chances in our own half and played more longer balls.' Nobody can dispute the great success that Charlton had with that team as he found a style that allowed Ireland to compete against higher-quality players. Kevin also suggests that Jackie was innovative in developing a pressing game. The downside of Jackie's approach to the game was evident in his decision to substitute Liam Brady after 35 minutes in a game against West Germany. This substitution prompted Liam to retire from international football. Liam Brady was a world-class playmaker, but apparently Jackie felt that Liam's presence was causing Ireland to 'lose control in midfield'. There is an obvious contradiction here; a manager wants control in midfield and yet substitutes his best footballer. What Jackie really wanted was to bypass his midfield.

Despite Jackie's success with Ireland, I maintain that managers who approached the game by missing out midfield did lasting damage to the game in England. Football teams need balance, but in England, by which I mean within the country at large, and also within the national squad, I strongly believe that it is time we concentrated

169

on developing players who can play out from the back and through midfield. Ultimately, this is the only way that we are likely to win a major tournament.

Glenn Hoddle was one of the best players I played against. Despite his injuries, 53 caps seems a poor return for a world-class player. In my view England should have built a side around Hoddle in the way that France did with Michel Platini and Zinedine Zidane. He had that rare ability to make time stop as he manipulated the ball while weighing up his options. He was a superb two-footed passer. Bobby Robson said that he couldn't pick Ray Wilkins, Bryan Robson and Hoddle in the same midfield. He also made the point that Hoddle wouldn't put his 'foot in'. Well, all I can say is that Hoddle would have been my first pick. Of course you wanted Hoddle for his ability to penetrate defences, but my experience of playing against him was that he was also prepared to work. I cannot understand why Ron Greenwood picked Glenn for his first international, then left him out for the next five. In many ways his elegance and passing ability reminded me of Beckenbauer. Why would anyone want to bypass a midfield with Hoddle in it?

There are certain players who managers should change their system for. At Juventus, Ancelotti realised that he would have to abandon his favoured 4-4-2 to play Zidane as a number ten behind the two strikers. Robson acknowledged that Hoddle was a highly gifted player, but mentions that he couldn't be relied on to track back or tackle. That wasn't my experience when playing against him, but even if he hadn't done the dirty parts of the game, why wouldn't you play a man who Arsène Wenger, when he signed him for Monaco, described as a 'magician'? Glenn achieved legendary status at Monaco, and is regarded as the greatest player in Monaco's history.

Unfortunately in England we didn't have enough defenders who were truly comfortable on the ball. We probably still don't. Even at international level, England didn't have defenders who could play the cute balls that Beckenbauer or Alberto played from the back. It is a pity that Rio Ferdinand and Hoddle didn't play at the same time. I strongly believe that there is great merit in the way Guardiola transforms midfield players into defenders. When Mascherano went from Liverpool to Barcelona, Guardiola converted him into a defender with great success. The future, at the highest level, lies with centre-backs who are comfortable on the ball, and who can play combinations against hard-pressing teams.

I played against Paul Gascoigne when he was very young and at Newcastle. He had massive confidence and ability to match it. His tight control and strength made it very difficult to get the ball from him, and he would draw players to him, leaving gaps for others to exploit. It is ironic of course that Hoddle brought Paul's international career to an end by not selecting him for the 1998 World Cup. I have heard that Hoddle's man-management skills were not the best, but if Gascoigne wasn't fit as a result of 'refuelling problems', Glenn probably had little choice. Gascoigne won four more caps than Hoddle, but both had world-class ability and should have earned more than they did.

It may not surprise the reader to find out that I believe the closest player to Gascoigne today is Jack Grealish. He is not in Paul's class yet. Of course I hope that Dean Smith keeps him, and develops Aston Villa into a good side; he certainly improved Jack in the 2019/20 season. I know that Jack can improve his defensive contribution but he has that same ability Gascoigne had – to draw opposing players to him, disrupting defences. He is a player who brings joy to the game. It also doesn't take a genius to see that Phil Foden has the potential to be a top international player, and I am looking forward to seeing him have more game time next season. We have some talented players eligible for England now. I hope Gareth Southgate keeps faith with that talent, although I fear that we are going to have to unearth some outstanding ball-playing defenders to get the best out of that talent.

7

Bingo! We're Down

WHEN RON SAUNDERS came to Albion, I needed to leave. I have never referred to Saunders as a bully, but when he called me 'Baldy', and said he didn't want ball players in the middle of the park, I felt that it was personal. It is the manager's right to pick and develop the team he wants to represent him and the club, but I had developed into a hard-working, passing midfielder and an England international. I would be named as Albion's player of the year for the 1985/86 season (this is probably unique, because I had already left the club when the vote took place). I knew he wasn't prepared to give me a chance.

Andy Blair and I signed for Villa in March 1986, and we both played a large part in saving that side from relegation. In retrospect it is obvious that we were firefighting. Stepping into the shoes of Villa's European Cup-winning midfield, with such a young side around us, was always going to be a big ask even if I didn't quite realise it at the time. Graham Turner, the manager, was young and comparatively inexperienced, but in *Ticket to the Moon* it is made clear that Deadly Doug Ellis was keeping a tight hold of the purse strings. Richard Sydenham provides a list of the players Turner wanted to buy. Included were Neil Webb, Gary Lineker, Alan Smith (then at Leicester), Terry Butcher, Richard Gough, and John Gidman. As Sydenham explains, Ellis 'would never place sentiment above financial logic'. Most of these targets were missed because Ellis wouldn't sanction the transfer fee or the wages.

I made my England debut at the same time as Lineker, and you didn't need to be a football genius to know that there was a ton of goals in him. Sydenham tells us that Turner made enquiries for Lineker but expected him to stay with Leicester. He didn't stay at Leicester and instead was sold to Everton for £800,000, then a year later Barcelona signed him for £2.8m. Richard explains that this was Turner's error of judgement, but it would not have surprised me to find that Ellis had baulked at the price. It was not 'financial logic' to fail to invest in players who might well have kept Villa in the First Division. Butcher, in particular, would have provided the leadership that Turner's team desperately needed; he was signed by Rangers for £725,000 at the age of only 28, when he was probably at his peak.

A reading of *Ticket to the Moon* confirms what I felt at the time – that Turner had been given a hospital pass. Villa had won the First Division and European Cup when Ellis was away from the club. It is clear that missing the glory years rankled, and having been ousted he was determined on his return to be all-powerful. He became the first paid director in the club's history and imposed a salary cut on the players. The effect of this was the rapid break-up of the European Cup-winning side.

There were rumblings for a long time about me moving to Villa, and eventually I was transferred for £90,000 with Darren Bradley going the other way as part of the exchange. In different circumstances I would have been happy to stay with Albion. I had thoroughly enjoyed my time at the club, but Saunders had made it clear I wouldn't get a game in midfield.

I didn't get off to a flying start at Villa Park in my second spell. My first game was against West Ham and after two minutes I scored an own goal. I am glad to say that I got my head up, and we ended up winning 2-1 with two goals from Steve Hodge.

One of my early games was away at Newcastle playing against a brilliant young Paul Gascoigne. After Tony Dorigo was sent off we somehow found the spirit to fight our way into the game. After missing a sitter I managed to volley an equaliser in the 80th minute. It is so important not to let your head go down after making a mistake. It should be on the first page of all coaching manuals, 'We all make mistakes. Keep trying.'

In that first season back at Villa we lost only once in the eight games immediately after my arrival. By the time Turner took over the European Cup-winning side had been dismantled, and the investment was in youth. Hodge, Dorigo, Mark Walters, Paul Elliot and Martin Keown were all young players with a great deal of potential, but they were not capable, at that early stage of their careers, of replacing greats like Des Bremner, Dennis Mortimer and Gordon Cowans. Gordon was possibly the finest player to pull on a Villa shirt. He was 27 when Villa sold him to Bari. It is true that Gordon had broken his leg, but I believe had Villa kept him the story may have been different. I think Graham bought me to provide a bit of experience after Cowans had gone.

My old mentor, Ron Wylie, was the coach, and I carried my form from Albion to Villa, and even if I do say so myself, I think I had a considerable influence on the fact that we stayed up. Andy Blair also had a big influence, those young players needed older heads, and Turner said I was the single biggest influence on the improvement. My period at Cosmos had made midfield my natural home.

Pelé and Beckenbauer taught me the importance of having the confidence to slow things down if necessary and I think that was a key element in our improvement.

Before I joined Villa they had just been knocked out of the Milk Cup by Oxford and the fans were very unhappy, but we had a good run and managed to stay in the First Division. I was proud of my role in helping the side stay up, and my performances were acknowledged by John Pearson of the *Birmingham Evening Mail*, who wrote, 'Steve Hunt's qualities of ball control, composure and precision passing have been the major reason in Villa's surge to safety.'

A little immodest of me to put that quote in, but I can't help hoping that Ron Saunders read it at the time. I had great hopes for the following season. We signed Neale Cooper, Martin Keown, and my old colleague and mate Garry Thompson. I played a part in the signing of Garry. On a close-season trip to Mauritius, Doug Ellis asked me to join him on the upper deck of the jumbo we were in. He asked me who I thought might be a good addition to the squad. I had no hesitation in mentioning Garry, and before very long he was at Villa Park. Garry was a quality striker, but his best years were at Coventry and Albion. His striking record wasn't great at Villa but I don't think he was helped by the lethargy that had crept into the team.

Martin Keown was not guilty of a lethargic approach. He was an intense, ambitious, talented young man who had stumbled into the shambles that Villa had become. He always seemed a bit of an outsider. Some players took the piss out of him for his failure to fit in. I felt he was misunderstood, and it must have been a shock for a young player to arrive at a club where morale was so low.

A 6-0 defeat against Nottingham Forest represented a new nadir. I felt that some players were not giving enough and were coasting through games. A few of them were looking to move. I had put in a transfer request at Coventry because I felt the club lacked ambition. Even after that request was turned down I played with full commitment, but that same level was missing in the Villa team at this time. I don't blame Graham Turner for this, but some players were not giving everything.

My optimism had been misplaced; we made a terrible start. Deadly Doug was not known for his patience and sacked Turner. Many players in that squad went on to have great careers but perhaps there was not quite enough experience, or perhaps there was an absence of the team spirit I had enjoyed at Coventry. It was probably a combination of the two. That 6-0 defeat at Nottingham Forest was Graham's last game and after it, Doug took Graham for a little walk round his garden where he kept his metaphorical flick knife concealed by the roses. Graham was a decent man and a good manager, and maybe the job came a little early for him. Excuse the cliché, but it was now a question of out of the frying pan and into the fire.

Graham went on to work wonders at Wolves, and I happen to think that he would have turned it around at Villa. His successor certainly didn't improve things.

Ellis was typical of those chairmen who get fixated on changing the manager. Sometimes they get it right, but more often than not they get it wrong. The classic example was the appointment of Gianfranco Zola at Birmingham City. Clearly, the Chinese owners wanted sexy football. You can put a scruffy man in an Armani suit and he will almost certainly still look scruffy, but he will also feel uncomfortable. Gary Rowett had built a pragmatic team of hard workers who were on the brink of the play-offs. The Zola experiment resulted in a relegation struggle which they only survived because Harry Redknapp saved them at the last minute. Deadly Doug was like a wayward husband forever casting glances at his mates' girlfriends. Are they better looking? Better company? Will my life improve if I change my wife? So he changes his wife, and for the first few days everything is rosy.

Billy McNeill's first game in charge of Villa was at Anfield. We were bottom of the league but amazingly we drew 3-3. Headlines like 'Villa Burn So Bright for Billy' and 'Horizon Looking Rosy' were, however, soon replaced by 'McNeill's Men Hit New Low' – on that particular occasion when Villa lost to Ipswich Town in the Full Members' Cup. In that relegation season there is no doubt in my mind that Billy was let down by some of the players. A tight dressing room is essential; you don't have to socialise with each other but you do have to play for each other. I am convinced that some players were not doing enough. Some of the players had their heads turned by interest from other clubs which damaged the spirit in the dressing room. The slightest drop in commitment affects results and team spirit. The atmosphere at the club wasn't great, but Billy seemed unable to change the mood.

Football can be a cruel world, and the humour is often from the school playground. I refer you to the incident of the mask. Piss-taking is at the heart of footballers' humour. Any slight oddness can be picked on, and young players soon have to develop a thick skin. One young player – a future international and an outstanding prospect – once knocked on the door of my hotel room in a distressed state. When I got him talking it turned out that he felt he didn't fit in, and he was concerned that people didn't like him. It didn't help his cause when he appeared at breakfast the next morning in a striking yellow jumper with the word 'Lemon' on it.

Footballers are not usually noted for sophisticated satire, and their sense of humour can be cruel, basic or unkind – or all three. The player simply had to develop a thicker skin, and of course, not wear a lemon jumper with 'Lemon' written on it. Come to think of it, don't wear lemon – with or without writing, unless you want to resemble a 1970s chat show host. You need a thick skin to be a footballer. At Coventry, Gerry Francis turned up in big-collared shirts and tank tops like a refugee from the early '70s. Gerry had captained England and been a top-class player. He could probably have got away with flares. Anyway, the man in the lemon jumper went on to have an outstanding club and international career. Just like Francis, he would have been able to indulge his liking for strange clothes after he had won his caps and medals.

As a veteran of fighting relegation in England, I can only state the obvious: the only way to survive is for every player to fight for every point. Peter Kay does a sketch in which he examines the daft things we all say, such as 'first things first' or 'is it hot in here, or is it just me?' It is part of a show called *Guess Who Died?* A woman called Connie has been run over by a bus. Her neighbour says, 'I only saw her last Tuesday. She looked fine to me.'

It is now a cliché to examine football clichés and daft comments, but that isn't going to stop me. 'It was a game of two halves.' Unfortunately, for some players it's not. Most footballers want to do their best, but I have played with some whose head went down after the first goal against their side. Some players simply accept the inevitability of defeat, and they stroll around waiting for the final whistle. I know why this is. When, in the 1980s Coventry had been beaten several times by Liverpool, it was easy to get a heavy feeling in the heart when the first Liverpool goal went in, even if it was early in the game. If I was in a side that won a point at Anfield I felt a bit like the late tennis player, Vitas Gerulaitis, who finally beat Jimmy Connors after 16 successive defeats to him. He then responded, 'Nobody beats Vitas Gerulaitis 17 times in a row.' I am going to fall into the world of managerial clichés again. There are no easy games, and six-pointer relegation battles are a nightmare to play in. You need a manager who can keep calm, and deliver his tactics with an air of quiet confidence and a sense of purpose. We had none of those ingredients in that particular relegation season.

There is a lot of bullshit talked in football. As soon as a manager buys new players, let's say they are centre-halves, the man whose position is threatened will be saying things like, 'Competition will be good for my game,' or, 'Nobody was challenging for my jersey and this has affected my performances.' I think I may even have said similar things myself. What they are really thinking is, 'I hope these blokes aren't any good.' Did Shakespeare write *Hamlet* because he was worried about a new young playwright on the block? Did my hero Springsteen write 'Born to Run' because a young hip guitarist and songwriter had arrived in New Jersey? The point I am making in such a curious, roundabout way, is that great footballers drive themselves on to great performances, and don't hide behind excuses when they play badly.

It should of course be a question of pride to do your best every week but I am afraid that too many members of that Villa side thought talent alone could turn things around. There has to be a pride in performance. It is very difficult to imagine someone like Kevin De Bruyne saying that he felt jaded because he didn't have any competition for his place. After leaving Chelsea, De Bruyne went to Wolfsburg. It must have been difficult maintaining his form after rejection from Chelsea. As well as his talent, he seems to have that drive and pride in performance that all great players have. I saw this kind of pride at close quarters in the great players at the Cosmos.

That relegation season under Billy McNeill was a huge disappointment to me and everybody who loved Aston Villa. I had been at the wrong end of the table for many years, and I can remember saying before the season started that anything below tenth place would be a failure. I recall saying that we were ready to mount a serious challenge for the title. A friend pointed out that I was obviously no Nostradamus. Well, I have no idea who Nostradamus played for, but it certainly wasn't Cosmos. I looked him up and discovered that Nos was not a fancy-dan midfield player, but a prophet. He did at least have the good sense to be a very vague prophet, so that his predictions could be applied to virtually any outcome. I should have taken a leaf out of his book and said something bland like, 'I think we'll do okay.' The words 'below tenth place' and 'failure' would come back to haunt me.

McNeill's spell at Villa was not a happy one. It was disappointing that a man of his stature in the game could not establish a sense of purpose. He was one of the Lisbon Lions, a great player and captain, and a legend in the game. His nickname was Cesar. I just thought this was a spelling mistake, and that the 'a' had been omitted by a Celtic supporter not *au fait* with Roman history. I am not myself a scholar of Roman history, in fact; as you may recall, I spent most history lessons gazing in longing at the goalposts in the recreation ground adjacent to the school. In the interests of authenticity I did some research into Julius Caesar, and discovered that he was made 'dictator perpetuo', which in football speak is the gaffer for life. Julius had obviously not met Deadly Doug Ellis. There was only one gaffer for life in Doug's world.

Apparently Julius had enormous power and influence. Billy had very little power or influence at Villa, and there was a total lack of purpose. He had a habit of saying the word bingo in team talks, 'Pass to him, and bingo it's a goal.' I used to call him Billy McBingo and his constant repetition of the word became a running joke among the players. Guardiola he wasn't. I can remember being so frustrated that I once poured a cup of orange juice over my own head at half-time. I think it was a spontaneous and desperate attempt to draw attention to the side's lack of direction. Billy seemed short of ideas, but in my view he also lost the dressing room. He may have been let down by the players, but his job was to turn things around at Villa. It's true that many of the players in the squad had their eyes on a move, but Billy was unable to change the culture. On one occasion before training Billy announced that he was going to impose fines on players who were booked. I simply refused to accept this and would not pay. My attitude was that if I was getting booked it was because of my commitment to the cause. There were some players in that side who could have done with showing a bit more commitment.

My son, Simon, who you will remember was inconsolable when I moved from the Albion to the Villa, soon became a

Villa fan. I suppose family loyalty runs deep. His obsession with Villa today is so complete that my other son, Jonathan, had to ban him from his pub for, let's call it 'overexcitement' when watching Villa. If a magical potion were to come along and transform my 64-year-old body and mend my dodgy knees, and if I then signed for Real Madrid, I'm pretty sure his loyalties would remain with Villa. It must have been very challenging for him in that 1986/87 season. He kept a scrapbook in which the following information has been completed: Favourite player? 'STEVE HUNT'. He reckons now it's in my handwriting, but I know it's his because my writing wasn't as good as my seven-year-old son's. Anyway, I am digressing. My point is that Simon doggedly wrote the scores down in that season. If you are a Villa fan, or that fool who hoped for a top ten finish, it makes very depressing reading.

Billy and Doug's honeymoon period was in October: they were on a tropical beach drinking cocktails, but in November and December marital tiffs about who did the washing-up and hoovering were undermining their relationship. By January, the divorce courts were preparing for another Deadly Doug divorce. Simon's scrapbook of results reads: 1 January – lost; 3 January – drew; 24 January – lost; 7 February – lost; 14 February – lost; 28 February – drew; 7 March – lost; 21 March – drew; 28 March – drew.

I think the Scottish players in particular were astonished to find how ineffective McNeill was. Allan Evans was more than disappointed with Billy. Allan was a towering figure at Villa and I know that he felt that McNeill simply would not accept any responsibility. If I hadn't known that Billy was a European Cup-winning captain, I would have been very surprised to be told that he had led Celtic to glory. He seemed totally lacking in leadership skills, and on one day consulted me, Andy Gray and Allan Evans, to ask our advice about what system of play we should employ. There is nothing wrong with the manager asking senior players about the way he wants to play, but McNeill seemed desperate and at a total loss.

There is an argument to suggest that good leaders will seek advice, but the team's morale was very low. We needed a manager who was willing to accept the responsibilities that come with leadership and at this time in his career Billy didn't seem willing to accept that responsibility. What's more, he didn't seem to have any real sense of commitment to the club or the city. For example, he was still living in Manchester. The club and team were struggling before McNeill's arrival but it was his job to motivate the players, or leave them out if they failed to fight. Graham Turner had relied on youth, so it wasn't Billy's fault that he inherited a young, unbalanced squad. Doug Ellis had a tight hold on the purse strings. That wasn't Billy's fault, although the one player he did buy, who he said would keep us up, was Warren Aspinall who came to us from Everton reserves. Warren was a good player but even Giorgio Chinaglia might have struggled to score goals in that Villa side. Billy failed to take responsibility for the poor performances and the subsequent low morale of the players.

We were relegated after taking 12 points from 30 matches, including a 5-0 defeat at Southampton in which we were 4-0 down at half-time. Our last game of the season was at Manchester United. Billy had been sacked, and my old youth team coach Frank Upton was in charge. We had already been relegated, but on that day I was captain and my son Simon was mascot. A bittersweet day captaining the club I had supported but with the knowledge that we were going down. I said I would shave off what little hair I had left which I did, and none has grown back. Five years after being European champions, Villa were relegated. Caesar was stabbed to death as a result of a plot by Cassius and Brutus. Cassius and Brutus had nothing on Deadly Doug, but in sacking Billy he made the right decision.

This research into Roman history has in fact been a waste of time, but I am going to leave it in as a form of apology to those history teachers at Perry Barr Comp who I failed to listen to. In fact, Billy's nickname at Celtic was

188

after Cesar Romero; the actor who played a getaway driver in *Ocean's Eleven*. The reason apparently was that Billy was the only Celtic player to own a car. Cesar Romero played the Joker in the TV series of *Batman*. It is tempting to say that the Joker might have made a better fist of managing Villa. I know Billy was a wonderful player, and a legend at Celtic, and I don't want to pick a fight with any proud Glaswegians who worshipped him, but I am certain that we would have been better off sticking with Graham Turner. Deadly Brutus Ellis replaced Billy with Graham Taylor. He was the right appointment for the club but his football philosophy was very different to mine.

Taylor was clearly the right man at the right time. I didn't like his style of play but he proved to be a very successful Villa manager and was able to develop a fighting spirit that, with some excellent signings, saw the team promoted and then finish second in their first season back in the First Division.

Taylor was a good club manager, but despite protesting that he didn't play a simple long-ball game, my experience of playing for him at Villa suggested he did. I can remember in a training session Graham coned off two sections of the pitch near the corner flags. The instructions were to hit those areas at every opportunity. He told the midfield players that, even when facing their own goal, they should try to hook the ball into the coned areas. There is no doubting Taylor's success at club level, but in my view the long-ball game did lasting damage to English football. From a player's perspective, I didn't spend hours working on my control in order simply to whack balls into the channels. It is a pleasure today to see the current young generation of English players being encouraged to express themselves.

Graham introduced afternoon training and started a more rigorous training regime. There is no doubt that he developed a winning culture at the club but I think I could tell that my knee wasn't going to hold out. I played 12 games in the Second Division that season. The team gained promotion, but I was going to have to cope with the loss of my passion and my living. After a career almost entirely in the top flight my playing days ended as they began, in the second tier.

8

I Should Have
Thought About That

I READ an article suggesting that footballers suffer from a high incidence of depression – not just after retirement, but also during their playing careers. Billy Kee was Accrington Stanley's leading scorer when he retired at the age of 29 to become a bricklayer. He had suffered from anxiety and depression; the game had driven him to a state of total despair, but early retirement had provided some relief and he explained, 'I could start living life how I wanted to without pressure from the fans, the managers and the relegations. If I hadn't opted out of the football world, I don't know if I would be alive now.'

I don't remember any of my colleagues talking about depression when they were playing, but pro football comes with its own pressure, and reading Alan Gernon's book –

Retired – about life after playing opened my eyes. I guess we never talked about these things then. For quite a bit of my career I was in teams battling relegation, and that can make playing an anxious experience. Sometimes I think the most fun you have in football is kicking about with your mates when you're a kid. My mate Dean and I used to spend hours kicking about on the underpass to the motorway in Perry Barr. Happy days.

I don't think I was depressed in my playing career but losing can seriously affect a player's mood, so you have to be careful not to let football interfere with family life. I suppose I was always driven by my desire to be a better player, to play for England, and here are those words again: to prove myself. I did get a buzz out of playing. I suppose the highs compensated for the lows. Once I had stopped playing I felt low. The buzz of playing had gone and I now believe that I was probably depressed. I don't think I was helped by what I perceived as a lack of support from Aston Villa, but I would suggest that simply the loss of that 'buzz' can have a bad effect on most players.

Clearly for some people, like Billy, the release from the pressure of the game outweighs that buzz. The phrase 'the buzz' is possibly overused. I would define it as a feeling of being completely alive when you are on the pitch. In some ways it appears inevitable that working-class, largely uneducated sportsmen, should be vulnerable to behavioural problems when that disappears. Top-class professional sport provides a heightened experience: it is hardly surprising that so many players after retirement turn to gambling, drink and drugs. Reading Paul Gascoigne's autobiography, it seems that without intense physical activity, he doesn't feel alive or even know what to do with himself. I have met somebody who knew him well. He told me that Gascoigne is a lovely guy, but that he had never met anybody more uncomfortable in his own skin. That lively, brilliant young footballer, who I played against early in his career, has struggled to maintain a stable life. There is no doubt in my mind that as a player he was touched by genius, but he required structured help earlier in his career.

I know it's ridiculous, but I had the idea that my playing days wouldn't end. Gernon's book assured me I wasn't alone. I never planned for retirement, so having to retire at 30 was a shock. Shortly after arriving at Villa I realised I was struggling with my knee. For some reason I didn't have a medical at Villa and looking back I wonder if I would have passed it. After a close-season tour during this second spell at Villa I went into the duty free shop and left with 500 cigarettes. I was a non-smoker. Why did I do it? I guess it was totally impulsive. Perhaps it was associated with the fact that I knew my career was coming to an end.

I had been in professional football for 14 years. Maybe the thought that I would soon no longer be able to do the only job I ever wanted to do led to me becoming a smoker at the age of 29. The routines and structures of a footballer's life, even in my day, were tightly regulated. The consequence of that impulsive gesture was that I became addicted to cigarettes. Fortunately, I managed to give up smoking when I started coaching kids, motivated by the imperative that a coach of young people should be a role model.

Writing this book has been a process of self-discovery. I have never quite worked out why I began smoking when I did. In his book, *Bottled*, Benjamin Roberts explains the thought process I must have been going through. I knew my knee would never be the same, and that retirement was imminent, 'In retirement, the conditions that the player has been suppressing throughout his career are now free to flourish.' In this context, Roberts indicates that the development of 'a smoking habit' is not unusual in players after retirement. At a time when I could have done with guidance and support, none was available. I was floundering – anticipating the loss of income, status and identity that would inevitably come after retirement.

So many players are affected by what Roberts refers to as 'adverse behaviour' that it is shocking to note that more support was not available to professional footballers when preparing for retirement. In the macho world in which I made my living it was not the done thing to talk about your fears for the future – about the loss of routine, excitement and income. Shortly after retirement I was invited to a party at a team-mate's house. It was a nice thought on the part of the host, but it was evident at the party that I was effectively an outcast. I don't blame my colleagues for that – it is clear that I represented their worst fears. Like me, and so many others, most of them would not have consciously anticipated the end of their careers.

Many players experienced addiction problems during their careers. Gascoigne's crude challenge on Gary Charles at Wembley probably caused both of their addiction problems to intensify. Charles became an alcoholic, but is now an expert in substance abuse helping footballers with addiction issues, both during their playing years and after retirement. In *Bottled*, Charles is quoted as having said that his alcohol issues would 'still be seen as a weakness now, in life and in sport', and Roberts writes, 'Can you imagine going to your boss and telling him you cannot stop drinking in the morning?'

Yet not only can it be imagined, but some employers have facilitated that exact situation. At Transport for London (TfL) a scheme was set up in which employees with addiction issues could report them without any fear of losing their job – provided they accepted help. Footballers live in constant fear of losing their job: of losing form, being dropped, going down the divisions, and subconsciously retiring. It is amazing to me now that I never spoke to anybody about the mental effect retirement had on me. Like many players, I tried hard to make a living in the game. I enjoyed some of the coaching, but if I am honest with myself it was a bad decision to go back into football. I was trying to replace 'the buzz', and it simply can't be done.

The jobs I have done outside football have given me greater stability and satisfaction. I work now as a primary school caretaker and feel part of a team working to provide the best environment for the kids to learn and play. If one current professional reads this, and starts to consider seriously the problems that may come with retirement, I will be as proud of that contribution as anything I ever achieved in the game.

The end came for me as it began at Villa – coming off injured in what was my last game. The cold reality came home to me after I went for a second opinion at Harley Street. The specialist told me that if I played again I would be a cripple. I had gone to London with the Villa physiotherapist, but needed some time on my own after this diagnosis. I wandered the streets in a state of confusion and despair.

I had probably lost a sense of my own identity when I retired. Looking back, I didn't give myself enough time to grieve about my retirement; I didn't really know how to grieve, or whether grieving was an appropriate response to no longer being able to play football. I guess speaking to somebody about my feelings would have helped. Still, I had to put food on the table, so I bought a van and started to make a living delivering building materials.

One bright spot was the fact that I had been assured by Graham Taylor that I would be 'looked after'. I hadn't heard from the club, and so made an appointment to see Graham at Bodymoor Heath. I turned up in my van, wearing my work overalls. The appointment lasted five minutes. Graham told me he had no influence in these matters and suggested I ring Doug Ellis. I had known Doug for many years, but in a brief phone conversation he told me that I should try Coventry or Albion for a testimonial; the feeble excuse given was that Villa fans would not look kindly on a man getting a testimonial from the club when he had spent a large part of his career at their West Midland rivals.

I am only 64, yet as a result of my injury, at a time when men of my age are playing tennis or running half-marathons, I would struggle to jog a few yards. When I retired I tried, without success, to gain compensation from an industrial tribunal. Coming to terms with a reduction in your mobility at such a young age is not easy. The football gods do not discriminate. Lifelong disability can be the outcome for a journeyman pro, or for a three-time Ballon d'Or winner like Marco van Basten. In his review of van Basten's autobiography, *Basta*, Donald McRae, writing in *The Observer*, describes how van Basten had to crawl to the bathroom in the middle of the night. The player had retired at the age of 30 having not played for two years. For a long time, van Basten had been playing through the pain in his ankles; poor medical advice and demanding managers caused him to push himself through the pain barrier. The outcome was that a young man of 30 could no longer walk to the bathroom. Marco's ankle was fused four years after retirement and although he is now pain-free, his mobility is limited.

I think my old manager, Johnny Giles, fully expresses the frustrations that many players experience when talking to club chairmen at the time of retirement or when leaving a club. In *A Football Man*, Giles – one of the greatest midfield players to play for Leeds, or in my view, any team – writes about how players of his generation had a naive expectation that their service would be rewarded. I know that my case was not the same as Johnny's, who made 525 appearances for Leeds over a period of 12 years. He was transferred to Albion having been informed that he would be paid £25,000 by Leeds in recognition of his service. Manny Cussins, the Yorkshire club's chairman, offered him £5,000. When John pointed out that he did not regard this as a fair settlement, Cussins's reply was, 'We paid you good money over the years.' John's reflections on this incident sum up my own feelings, 'What he was telling me was that I was being an idiot. I had served my purpose and these smart men were going to do nothing they weren't strictly obliged to do.'

I know that I did not have John's case, but I suppose that having been a supporter and an apprentice, making money for the club when they sold me to Cosmos, and having come back and played a big part in saving the team from relegation under Graham Turner, that having been forced to retire, and losing perhaps five years of wages, Aston Villa might have offered more support. In a scrapbook of my Coventry years I came across a magazine interview. I was asked what I would do when I stopped playing. My answer, 'I guess I had better start thinking about that.' Stupidly, I never did. That doesn't excuse the abrupt manner with which Doug Ellis dismissed my claim.

Pelé scored more than 1,250 goals in his career in professional football and was the greatest player in the world. I like to think that I am a realist, and I didn't expect a glittering finale in front of 75,000 people as I chanted 'love, love, love', but I couldn't help but remember Pelé's retirement game as I limped back to the van after leaving Graham Taylor's office. In fact I can assure you that the word love was nowhere near my lips as I journeyed home.

This post-retirement rejection was hard to take. Villa had promised to look after me, but instead I had to rely on my closest friend. Dean organised a benefit year with the help of a few other people who he makes reference to later in the book. I was extremely grateful for this support. The benefit year raised £8,000 with which I bought another van. Yet I felt there was a meanness in Villa's response, and was reminded of my debut for the club when a friend, Nicky Platts, ran on the pitch and virtually ripped the shirt from my back as a memento. Ron Saunders made me pay for the shirt.

Like a Dog Listening to Opera

Making a living from football was not the first thought on my mind after retiring, but Willenhall Town got in touch and so began my coaching career. My early experiences were positive: I enjoyed my time at Willenhall, and when Port Vale approached me about a coaching job, I felt positive about continuing a career in football. On the coaching staff at Port Vale were Mike Pejic and John Rudge, who both helped me learn a lot.

I have a vivid memory from my days at Port Vale of playing Manchester United in an FA Youth Cup game. They had a winger with a growing reputation, and I asked my full-back to get tight on him. The plan was working well. The United winger's name was Wilson, and he was quiet until the last 15 minutes in which he destroyed us. He was just brilliant. That winger later changed his name to Giggs. Ryan Giggs, or Ryan Wilson, as he was then, was exceptional. Few who saw him play as a youth could have had any doubts that here was a boy who was a star in the making.

I attended a Lilleshall coaching course at the height of the Charles Hughes nonsense. There is no doubt that the FA at this time was dysfunctional. The Hughes football model was an ugly blot on the game. It is strange to say the least that Bobby Robson didn't confront Hughes about his so-called winning formula. Look back at the 1974 World Cup, and the fluency and the art of that great Dutch side. Examine the brilliant Brazilian performances of four years previously. Watch again the pure genius of Xavi, Iniesta and Messi as they perfected their beautiful short passing game for Barcelona. Having watched all that, attempt to construct an argument in favour of *The Winning Formula*, the Charles Hughes coaching manual.

I understand that there are different ways of playing, and I understand that there are managers like Graham Taylor and Tony Pulis who worked hard to develop squads which played to their strengths. The bottom line, however, is that at the elite level direct football is inadequate. We should have been going in the direction of controlling possession when I did my course. I know that international sides have had success with less possession and a swift counter-attacking style, but the direct play Hughes was advocating had no chance. Why didn't Robson as England manager, and a man who believed in passing football, tell the great and good at the FA that the five-pass notion was nonsense? I can remember a load of graphs 'proving' that most goals were scored after fewer than five passes. Tell that to Pelé.

I played along with it because I needed to get the qualification. It reminded me a bit of the driving test: follow the instructions and then carry on in your own way. Tony Currie, a fellow student at Lilleshall, wasn't minded to follow the instructions; he thought that the five-pass principle was anti-football, and didn't hide it. He was happy to let the coaches at Lilleshall know what he thought. On one occasion, Currie dozed off at the side of the pitch while one of the Lilleshall staff was giving us the benefit of his knowledge. During Tony's own practical coaching session he stopped play and made his point in his unique way, 'Never mind all this rubbish. Just do this.' He then smashed a ball into the top corner of the net from 30 yards. He failed the course.

I still have the syllabus for the Lilleshall course. It was run by Davy Burnside, who made 127 appearances for Albion between 1957 and 1962. Burnside was known for his brilliant ball juggling – even performing his tricks at half-time during a friendly against CDSA Moscow. Now I know that freestyle football and ball juggling are separate activities, but I can't help wondering why a man who loved the ball enough to develop advanced juggling skills should want to peddle the dogma of *The Winning Formula*. A brief glance at the syllabus shows me that the course was entirely based on Hughes's book. Why did nobody seek to put Hughes right? By the time England failed to qualify for the World Cup in America in 1994, the hocus pocus delivered at Lilleshall had been found out. At the highest level Graham Taylor's long-ball tactics had been inadequate.

Let Pelé have a word on this matter through his biographer, Harry Harris. In 1994, Harris went to meet Pelé after England had failed to qualify, 'Pelé recommended a complete overhaul of the structure of the game in England, starting with a change in our philosophy. Pelé wanted "to spread the gospel of the beautiful game".' He would not have found it at Lilleshall, and neither did I or Tony Currie.

In his autobiography, Nobby Stiles writes about how he took exception when Hughes told him and his fellow learners at Lilleshall that West Germany scored their late equaliser against England in the 1966 final because there were too many men in the wall. It had been Nobby's responsibility to line up the wall and to check that Gordon Banks was happy. He was. Nobby was about to tell Hughes what he thought when his friend, sensing an eruption, warned him, 'to put your f*****g hand down if you want to get your coaching badge'.

In Jonathan Wilson's biography of Brian Clough he writes that Clough regarded the Hughes approach to coaching as 'primitive'. Like me, Clough had first-hand experience of Hughes at an FA coaching course. In a demonstration, Wilson tells us, Clough glanced a header with the side of his head into the bottom corner of the net. Instead of praising the finely judged, delicate finish, Hughes stopped the session to tell Clough that he should always head with the meat of the forehead, because that is where the bone is strongest, and from which the most power could be generated.

I admired Bobby Robson for his many achievements in the game. He was clearly an outstanding manager and a true football man, but I believe that he didn't speak out against Hughes because he didn't want to rock the establishment boat.

In the 1960s and '70s, the remnants of Victorian gentility were still to be found in small family businesses –

for example, when three brothers ran a company they would often seek to be referred to by their Christian names with the prefix 'Mr', presumably so that their employees did not get too familiar. Maybe it is a generational thing, but it stuck in my throat when reading Robson's autobiography, that he refers regularly to the old Etonian Cobbold brothers – who ran Ipswich Town – as Mr John and Mr Patrick. He tells a story about how John Cobbold was invited to become president of the South East Counties League. By Bobby's own admission, John knew little about football – presumably the ideal prerequisite to be president of the South East Counties League, and perhaps to access a seat on an FA committee. In his capacity, John, accompanied by Bobby, was due to gave a speech at a London hotel. I will let Bobby continue to tell the story, only pausing to let you know that the Ipswich chairman was pissed, 'When he stood up he swayed, closed his eyes and sank gracefully to the floor. He disappeared under the table and never said a word. He was carried out to a standing ovation – the applause was prolonged and thunderous. What an inaugural speech! What style! What class!' What bullshit!

In *Fawlty Towers*, Basil Fawlty fawns over a conman who is pretending to be a peer of the realm. 'What style! What class!' he keeps repeating, as the conman takes his money. By all accounts, John Cobbold was a very nice chap, but these local toffs had too much power in the game and at the FA.

Charles Hughes was a grammar school boy – an amateur structuring a coaching course for a game played mainly by working-class secondary school kids. Perhaps his grammar school background helped in retaining his grip on the job, but why on earth did Robson not assert himself? Robson was a football man, an expert, a professional who writes in his autobiography about how, with kindred spirits, like Dave Sexton, he agreed on the importance of passing, possession and control. Bobby even refers to Hughes making the ludicrous statement that, 'the Brazilians were doing it all the wrong way because they were all pass – pass – pass'. Despite this complete disagreement over football principles, Bobby seems quite proud of the fact that they 'never fell out' over their disagreements. I would contend here that not only should Robson have fallen out with Hughes, he should have offered to resign if the FA continued to allow Hughes to his wrecking ball at passing football. At a time when the FA should have been establishing the principles of Brazilian and Dutch football in the English game, Robson was passively standing by, 'Charles could debate and talk and put over his ideas.' What style! What class!

It doesn't at all surprise me that Alf Ramsey, a working-class man, had elocution lessons. He clearly wanted to be heard and seen as a gentleman, and despite his apparent contempt for the FA, he clearly wanted to fit in with the blazers. Can anyone imagine Brian Clough taking elocution lessons or putting up with the Hughes nonsense? I have been critical of Ron Saunders from a personal point of view but I must give him full credit for winning his battles with Deadly Doug. You can say what you like about Saunders (and I have), but he would not be cowed by the patronising types at the FA. Neither would Kevin Keegan.

I do sometimes wonder what the long-ball merchants think when they watch Manchester City or Barcelona in their pomp. A friend told me about a comedian called Stewart Lee. Stewart tells a story in his show about how the actor and presenter James Corden congratulated him on his show. Corden seems an engaging kind of guy, but Lee finishes the story by saying, 'James Corden watching me. It's like a dog listening to an opera.' I like dogs, but I have never taken mine to an opera. In fact my dog has been to the same number of operas as me. The comparison has stayed with me. Long-ball merchants watching Manchester City: it's like a dog listening to opera.

Arsène Wenger refers to football as a collective art. He talks about it from the perspective of the spectators, and suggests that for true lovers of football a game that captures the imagination and the emotions can be re-lived many years later. For example, I can still remember first seeing George Best play at the Hawthorns and marvelling at his grace and fluency. In my mind's eye those six goals he scored against Northampton are still present. Carlos Alberto's goal in 1970 still holds a place in my imagination – as does Pelé's brilliant dummy. Wenger is right: football should capture the imagination. His 2003/04 side came to be known as 'the Invincibles', reflecting their 49-match unbeaten run, but it is not the statistics that I remember, rather it is watching Robert Pires, Dennis Bergkamp and Thierry Henry performing their magic.

Tony Currie was another player who thought his career would defy time, and once said, 'I thought I could play the game I love forever.' He was a fabulous player who should have gained more caps. Trevor Hockey, whose boots I cleaned at Villa, once said that his instructions when playing with Tony at Sheffield United were to 'give the ball to Currie'. I felt that Tony was frustrated by the short-sighted insularity of the coaching dogma at Lilleshall.

It isn't as though the evidence was lacking that English football was ill-equipped to provide a successful international side. The Total Football of the Dutch team in the 1970s was signposting the way forward. In 1977 Holland beat England 2-0 at Wembley. The score didn't flatter the Dutch, who were playing a different game.

The then-England manager, Don Revie, had recognised that English football had to change, and had declared, 'There must be a realisation that what we produce at home every Saturday is not ideal for international competition.' When Revie left, Ron Saunders was spoken of as a possible candidate. Ron clearly had many strengths as a club manager, but his instincts were insular and represented the antithesis of what I learned playing with Beckenbauer and Pelé. Saunders had an innate suspicion of continental style influencing British football. It was this kind of attitude that helped keep Charles Hughes in charge of the FA coaching system for so long, and which eventually saw Graham Taylor ill-advisedly appointed as England manager.

No Weetabix For Me

I enjoyed my time at Port Vale, but when Leicester City came calling it seemed too good an opportunity to miss. The manager was Brian Little, who I had played with and who I had known for a long time. Also on the staff was Allan Evans who had been my room-mate at Villa and a good friend. Although I was looking forward to the job, I don't think I had fully recovered from the shock of early retirement. It was also at a time when my marriage to Sue was under strain. In his book, *Retirement*, Alan Gernon outlines a common pattern for professional footballers:

retirement, depression, marital breakdown. I didn't realise it at the time, but my life seemed to be following that typical course.

On leaving the marital home I moved in with another member of the Leicester coaching staff, David Nish. I was consumed by the usual strains connected with marriage breakdown, but my clear priority was to be a good father to my children, Simon, Natalie and Jonathan. The collapse of my marriage was accompanied by an inevitable strain on finances. I was determined to provide for my family and approached Little for a rise to help with the rent money. Little was accommodating, using the same words that Graham Taylor had, 'We'll look after you, Steve.' The rent money never arrived.

John Gregory, who was also on the staff at Leicester, and who eventually became Villa manager, moved in with me and David. This arrangement did not end happily. I learned from members of the first team that Gregory had been making disparaging remarks behind my back. He may have thought it was harmless or a laugh; I suppose I didn't see the funny side. I told him he had two hours to clear his stuff out of the house. We haven't spoken since.

The youth team I managed was going well, and had reached the final of the Midland Cup. The opponents were to be Aston Villa. I was beginning to feel some resentment about what little attention was given by the senior management to the youth team. On two occasions Brian Little interrupted my sessions, and on the second of those it was to clear snow off the pitch at Filbert Street. It seemed to me that Little wasn't interested in the work I was doing. My star player at the time was Julian Joachim who was on the fringes of Leicester's first team. I can understand why Brian wouldn't want Joachim to be injured playing for my team, but it was still a blow when he said he couldn't play in the final, and would have to be on the bench against Villa. Leicester lost on penalties.

It was my responsibility to tell players that they wouldn't be getting a professional contract. It was a particularly painful part of the job, and I always recalled receiving that letter from Neville Briggs telling me I wouldn't get my apprenticeship at Villa. One young player I was impressed by was Tony Thorpe. Unfortunately the powers that be decided that he was too injury-prone, saying he had glass ankles. I am glad to say that Tony became a prolific striker for Luton Town and Bristol City. Joachim was the most talented player in that group at Leicester. He had electric pace and masses of ability, but I felt that he wasn't quite the finished article and was thrust into the first team too early. Julian played for England at every level except full international level. He was an outstanding talent. He should have gained full England caps. Perhaps that talent should have been nurtured for a little longer.

A sense of disillusionment was settling on me. Matters weren't helped by the fact that Little had not provided the extra money that had been promised. Of course this may not have been his fault. My relationship with the chairman was a little shaky. Martin George was a member of one of the richest families in England – but I found him patronising. He asked me in a rude manner to shave off my beard for a club photo. I had confronted Giorgio Chinaglia and Pelé at the age of 20 so I was not prepared to be spoken to as though I was a schoolboy, and I was not going to shave it off at the request of George. I was not surprised that, in his autobiography, Emile Heskey expresses the view that he was bullied by George into signing his first contract. Leicester did at least provide me with one big positive: a new relationship. I started dating Kirsty, who worked in the club office. We have now been married for 25 years.

My relationship with George did not improve. The day after the annual club ball, George gave me the benefit of his sartorial advice, 'My wife thought you'd slept on a bench the night before the ball, and you're still wearing that beard.' Martin George was the Weetabix tycoon. I used to like Weetabix but I haven't eaten it since. Perhaps this shaky relationship with the chairman had an effect on the events that followed.

My sense that my work wasn't being appreciated was reinforced when, with the youth team about to embark on a trip to a tournament in France, not one of the senior management team came down to wish the lads well. The team came third. When I returned from the tournament, Kirsty suggested visiting her parents, holidaying at a campsite in the South of France. I jumped at the chance and asked for permission to use one of the club's cars. After a long drive through France we were looking forward to a relaxing couple of weeks. We were very close to the campsite when, after turning a bend, we were confronted by a vehicle on the wrong side of the road. The car ended up in a ditch and we both needed hospital treatment.

The injuries were minor, but it had been a shock; the car unfortunately was a write-off. As the accident had clearly not been my fault, and as I had gained permission to use the car, I was not unduly concerned about informing the club. When I phoned up I was shocked to find that they appeared more concerned about the car than about our welfare. After this call I became very angry.

I think there had been a lot of anger building up over the years and I didn't know how to deal with it. I no longer had playing to focus on and had not found a way to process what

I now regard as a lengthy period of depression. Meeting Kirsty had changed my life but I was still failing to express my feelings and, embarrassingly, on this occasion I failed again to control my anger.

My first thought after the call was to go to the bar. We were staying on a caravan site with Kirsty's family and after going into the caravan to announce that I was heading for the bar, my anger got the better of me: I slammed the caravan door and shattered a window in the process. I was in an incredibly low mood sitting in that bar, but was rescued by Kirsty's dad Robin, who was a model of support and understanding. My sleep that night was fitful and my feelings fluctuated between anger and remorse. I felt embarrassed about the prospect of facing Kirsty's family in the morning and, having woken early, I went straight out. I don't know if it has any psychological significance but I found myself sitting down, leaning on a goalpost of a football pitch on the site.

It was Kirsty's mum, Christine, who found me there. She was wonderful and I was very grateful for the calm, understanding manner of both parents. Christine managed to talk me down and calm me a little.

At this stage my heart was no longer in the holiday. The unsympathetic response to my phone call should have set alarm bells ringing, but I simply thought I had better get back to work. It was a surprise to arrive at Leicester railway station to find my old Villa room-mate, and Leicester colleague, Allan Evans, waiting for me. 'The gaffer wants a word, Steve,' he said. As soon as I entered Brian Little's office I knew that something was up. From the far corner of the room, Little announced, 'I'll have to let you go.'

My friend Dean tells me that I can be unforgiving. Dean is a 'water under the bridge' type of person, but I know I am not like that. It is a matter of trust; if I feel someone has let me down I find it hard to forgive and forget. It is possible that my experiences with my dad shaped me, and when I rejected his attempt to reconcile, it established a pattern of behaviour. I felt let down at Leicester City especially when, after my dismissal, Kirsty started to experience difficulties at her job. I felt that the chairman had his knives out for me. And my beard! People who I regarded as friends capitulated.

Alan Gernon writes about a young professional player called Shane Supple. Shane was on the books of Ipswich Town when he decided that a career in football wasn't for him. Some 'people in the game were yes men that would do anything to keep themselves in a job', according to Gernon. I am no angel, but nobody could accuse me of being a yes man; my instinct is to support my friends. I felt let down at Leicester where I was working 60 hours a week and believed I was doing a good job. Trust is important to me. For better or worse, I guess I'm not a 'water under the bridge' type of person, and I was disillusioned with the professional game.

Professional football consumes your identity. I have always had good relationships with family and close friends outside the game, but it is difficult to convey to a layman how a missed chance or a fluffed pass can play over and over again in your mind. It is also true that for me there was nothing quite the same as professional football for providing pure adrenaline. I now know that having another passion from which I could have earned a living would have helped. I have always had a passion for music. I guess a psychoanalyst would say I replaced my football obsession with Springsteen. You can't, however, make a living out of attending Springsteen concerts; in fact, you need a decent living to go to concerts these days.

My big mistake was going back to football to earn a living because while I enjoyed some aspects of coaching, it never replaced playing. Family and friends encouraged me to earn my money from the game, but even when teaching kids, an aspect of coaching which I generally enjoyed, there was too much hassle. I managed to get a job in the States, coaching kids at a football summer camp which I thought would provide a good opportunity to experience the US with Kirsty. They housed us in a small bungalow with no air conditioning, and it seemed to me that the established coaches were hogging all the better players. I didn't enjoy the experience, and in an echo of the hot-tempered young man who had arrived in New York in 1977, I threw a crate of soft drinks across the tarmac as I left.

Despite my dissatisfaction, there were lighter moments in the camp. When I first went to America, Sue and I experienced a real sense of culture shock with the language itself often providing problems. I clearly still hadn't mastered American colloquial expressions. I was in the middle of a shooting drill when a young girl came up to me and asked, 'Coach Steve! Do you mind if I do some shagging behind the goal?' I asked her to hold on a minute, and went to consult one of the American coaches. Through tears of laughter, he explained that 'shagging' meant 'to round up the balls behind the goal'.

On the whole, I found coaching outside the professional game much more of a positive experience. I enjoyed coaching island kids at the local high school as they were generally responsive and eager to learn. It was a relief to be away from the politics of most professional clubs. I was helped in my coaching on the island by a guy called Tommy Power, who had asked me if I needed any help as he wanted to learn from me – he also wanted to take his coaching badges. It was my good fortune that I agreed; Tommy was a great help to me. He became a great coach and a good friend.

My experience of coaching outside the professional game in England was tarnished by two unfortunate assignments. One puzzled me; the other was, without my knowledge, illegal, and resulted in me having to give evidence for the prosecution in a fraud trial. Let me first deal with the puzzling case. I was approached by a former footballer who worked in the community for Bournemouth. He asked me if I was interested in coaching a team to represent Bournemouth in the Community in a community league. It would be an under-18 team based on the Isle of Wight, and the players would attend Isle of Wight College to gain a football qualification. The strange aspect of this was that although there were some Isle of Wight boys and some from the mainland, many came from abroad, including from Australia and Russia.

I felt sorry for these boys as the sessions took place in local recreation grounds. It was soon apparent that the boys had been sold a dream of professional football. I don't know who was responsible for selling these dreams or whether the young men had just got carried away. What I did know was that the boys didn't have the ability to make it in the professional game. They were, however, generally of a goodish standard and the team was competitive, but the boys were unhappy, and I don't blame them. To travel halfway around the world to train on a local recreation ground is not acceptable. I can only think that some of the boys had stars in their eyes. Three of the more able players went to Bournemouth for trials, but the longest any of them stayed was six months. I am not blaming the club, but there was very little support, and the scheme felt exploitative, although I have no idea what the motive could have been. I was glad when I was able to put this project behind me.

One evening, I received a knock on my front door from a man who introduced himself as a member of the Serious Fraud Squad. He had come to the island from London. My first instinct was to ask him if he had come to the right house. When he explained that he was investigating Luis Michael Training Ltd, I realised he had indeed come to the right place.

I had been approached by a former professional footballer to provide a course on football coaching for 16- to 19-year-olds. They had been told they were doing an apprenticeship in NVQ activity leadership, which would pave the way to a football coaching career. I was hired as a tutor, along with Neville Southall, and other ex-players, to deliver the training. Almost 150 professional and semi-pro clubs were lured into the scheme.

The fraudsters had persuaded nine colleges to employ Luis Michael Training as a sub-contractor, using government cash to deliver apprenticeships. The people who ran Luis Michael Training received £5m of public money selling football dreams to vulnerable young men who received next to no training. Many of the youngsters ended up sweeping changing room floors or selling match programmes. The fraudsters extracted the money from the Skills Funding Agency, and pocketed a large part of the cash. Many who were enrolled on the scheme only received a couple of hours' relevant training a week. They had been promised 30 hours. Eventually, the fraudsters simply created false identities, and gained money for boys who didn't exist: as many as 30 per cent of names registered were made up.

It made me feel sick to think of the kids who were sold this false dream, and although giving evidence in court was an uncomfortable experience, the perpetrators deserved their sentences. The beautiful game is sometimes not so beautiful. In truth, I tried to put these experiences behind me, and prefer to think of Pelé trying an outrageous overhead kick, Beckenbauer splitting a defence with the outside of his foot, or Bogie tormenting the opposition.

It wasn't until I became established working in a hardware store, and most recently as a school caretaker, that I realised I was much happier making a living outside of football. Developing an identity beyond that bubble is difficult if it has been your passion and your only job. My advice, even to the wealthy superstars of the Premier League, is to start thinking about what you want to do when you finish playing, and not to expect to replace the playing buzz with coaching and management.

9

Sweet FA and Other Matters

KEVIN KEEGAN didn't give up the England job because he wasn't good enough. He gave up because the FA was not fit for purpose. After acknowledging that 'there were some good people working hard behind the scenes who wanted to move the organisation into the 21st century', he went on to describe the FA, in the time he was England manager, as 'an old boys' network that was completely set in its ways and appeared to be stuck in a time warp'.

As further evidence of this FA time warp, let us look at their sorry history in relation to women's football. I wrote earlier in this book of my sense of pride that, in some small way, I may have played a role in encouraging grassroots football for girls and boys in America. Until comparatively recent times the FA could not have said the same. In his definitive history of women's football, *Girls with Balls*, Tim Tate writes that it wasn't until 1988 that the FA allowed mixed football for under-11s and that it took until 1992 for it to abandon its hostility towards the women's game. So, not only did the FA do nothing for women's football, it was actively hostile towards it.

We can go back to Kevin Keegan to find out why the FA did so little to encourage girls and women to play football. Kevin observed that some of the committee members 'reminded me of the people you might find running the seniors competition at your local golf club'. It is not too fanciful to suggest that the people who discouraged women from becoming full members of golf clubs were the same ones who discouraged half of the population from playing the beautiful game. FA committee members were constrained by their conservative instincts. Their default position was to oppose reform and resist the social advances made in the latter part of the 20th century. They were, for the most part, defenders of the establishment, keen to appoint managers who would preserve the status quo. Kevin was clearly not that man.

The FA has improved in some ways but is still not entirely fit for purpose. After investing heavily for many years in futsal – the game that has developed so many great Brazilian players – the FA in their wisdom has decided to withdraw virtually all funding for the sport. In a letter to *The Guardian* on 20 October 2020, Leanne

Skarratt, the founder and captain of Manchester Futsal Club's women's team, writes, 'Over the past seven years I have watched my sport grow from strength to strength. Participation has grown exponentially at grassroots level for women and girls.' The FA has announced that it will lose £300m in lost income over the next four years, but as Leanne points out, 'Cuts to futsal will only recoup a measly £900,000.' As yet, the FA has not responded to the futsal community. I will leave the last words on futsal to Leanne, 'We need answers as to why our governing body – the wealthiest football association on the planet – has almost completely abandoned us at a time when our sport was taking flight.'

Academies

It was Howard Wilkinson who developed the idea of the academy system. The intention was to hand the development of talented young players to the professionals, and train young players with professional guidance, and within the best facilities. Although I believe the clubs take kids too early, I have some sympathy with Howard's original vision. By his own admission, however, his well-laid plans have been undermined by many of the clubs with devastating consequences for the mental health of rejected young players.

On 10 October 2017, in an interview with David Conn in *The Guardian*, Howard stated that top clubs were failing in their 'moral responsibility' by not giving enough young English players the chance to succeed. It has been well documented that an overwhelming majority taken on by the professional clubs do not make a career in the game. This is not unique to this generation; I believe that I was the only member of my Villa boys team to gain an apprenticeship and make a career in professional football. A big difference today, however, is the added air of intensity from parents. Expectations are often heaped on the kids, who invariably suffer from mental health issues when they are rejected.

Howard's view is that the clubs themselves are also culpable, because there isn't a real commitment to giving the kids an opportunity to succeed. This lack of commitment has major implications for the kids, but it also has implications for the game at national level. Wilkinson believes, as I do, that the reliance on overseas stars means that too few English players get the opportunity to play at the highest level. Howard refers to research which suggests that, to have a chance of succeeding, a national team must have at least 50 players with high-level experience, including in the latter rounds of the Champions League.

Football and Dementia

Football can consume identities in much more devastating ways than I have described earlier in this book. As I write this, Andy Bull in *The Guardian* on 24 October 2020, is reporting that Dr Judith Gates, who is married to ex-Middlesbrough centre-half Bill Gates, is involved in a campaign to find some definitive answers to the possible links to dementia and heading a football. Many players of my generation and before have dementia, and there appears to be a disproportionate proportion of footballers with the disease. In *The Telegraph*, Jeremy Wilson refers to a study by Dr Willie Stewart, which established that there was a five-fold increased risk of Alzheimer's for professional footballers. Bill Gates has been diagnosed with Chronic Traumatic Encephalopathy (CTE), which is directly linked to traumatic blows to the head – the sort of blows received by centre-halves repeatedly heading balls out of their box.

Dr Gates's campaign is designed to establish independent research that influences future practice so as to 'protect future generations'. This campaign has the support of Jack Charlton's widow Pat, and Nobby Stiles's son Rob, and granddaughter Caitlin. Sadly, Nobby died in the week I was writing this passage. Understandably, many have paid tribute to Nobby's dance with the Jules Rimet Trophy, and his wonderful career, rather than the dementia he had been suffering from for nearly 20 years. I hope, however, that someone takes notice of Caitlin Stiles's dissertation, 'The increased risk of neurodegenerative diseases in UK professional football – should football governing bodies respond?'

There is now an overwhelming case for independent research. 'Independent' is the key word here because Dr Gates argues, according to Andy Bull, that the Concussion in Sport Group (CISG) – the most influential organisation in determining good practice – may not be truly independent. Her argument is that a large majority of the CISG panel are connected to sporting organisations which have a vested interest, usually economic, in a conservative approach, to the possible links between CTE and sport. Now that both Jeff Astle and Alan Jarvis have been found to have died from industrial disease as a result of playing football, it is the very least we should expect, that future generations are protected.

The PFA

In 2020, Gordon Taylor, the chief executive of the PFA, receives a salary including bonus and benefits of more than £2m. He is about to step down from this lucrative job after 39 years. Taylor is not a here-today-gone-tomorrow union leader; it is sobering to think that by the time I retired, 35 years ago, Taylor had been in charge of the PFA for almost the entire duration of my career in England. Having the highest-paid union official in the world is not a good look for the PFA, which represents a lot of struggling ex-players and players on modest salaries in lower divisions.

It is true that today the PFA offers a wide range of support for some of the problems that footballers face, but even though the PFA 'is extremely proud to offer continued support and funding to the Sporting Chance clinic', it is quite astonishing that it was left to an individual – Tony Adams – to set up that clinic. The central point I am making here is, what on earth was the PFA doing about addiction issues before 2000? Why did players have to wait for a motivated and inspiring individual to have to set this up?

It must have been evident even when Taylor started the job in 1978, that there was a need to support players for addictive behaviour, and the wide range of issues that affect retired footballers. When I retired through injury the support offered by the PFA was minimal.

An independent review of the PFA was conducted by Naomi Ellenbogen QC. Taylor has so far failed to publish it in full. Why? His members have a right to see it. Taylor only agreed to this review after 300 ex-players pressed for reform of the organisation. It was Ben Purkiss, the PFA chairman, who exerted pressure on the organisation to agree to this review. Apparently, the PFA response was to question his membership because he was a non-contract player with Walsall. There is one overriding question which must be answered by this review. Given its vast reserves of money, is the PFA spending enough on the welfare of players and ex-players? In addition to issues of addiction, we know that a disproportionate number of ex-players suffer from dementia, depression and debt, and often a range of physical problems connected to their playing career. Why not publish this review in full, Mr Taylor?

It's a Better Game Now

Wimbledon under Dave Bassett and Bobby Gould were successful. Nobody can deny that. Reaching the top division of English football, and later winning the FA Cup, was a fairytale story. The only problem was that the football was brutal and crude. Balls were launched into space for John Fashanu and his colleagues to chase. It is said that they won the cup because Liverpool were intimidated by their physicality after Vinnie Jones felled Steve McMahon just a few seconds in to the 1988 final. There is a thin line between physicality and brutality; Wimbledon crossed that line. At Villa Park in my second spell at Villa I chased a ball down the left. I could feel a presence behind me and instinctively I knew it was Jones. I anticipated his challenge, which could have broken my leg, and I jumped in the air. I landed on his chest as he slid through to the cinder track. I soon found myself being hoisted in the air by Fashanu. 'I'll break your f…..g legs next time,' said Jones.

There is a view, widely expressed, that men's football isn't a man's game these days. It is a view expressed largely by people who have never been confronted by a player who thinks nothing of inflicting grievous bodily harm on an opponent. It was common to receive an elbow in the face and for the culprit to remain unpunished. I can remember being elbowed in the mouth by Everton's Gary Stevens, and nearly choking on the two front teeth that had been knocked down my throat. When I visited the dentist, expecting the stubs to be capped or to be fitted with a plate, I was asked to deliver the teeth to him when they appeared from the lower part of my anatomy.

Playing in my day was a test of having the mental strength to want the ball when you knew that the opposing player was interested only in maiming you. I have just watched clips of a game I played for Coventry against Manchester City. Half of the players would have been sent off today. Of course, great players like George Best had to put up with the kind of treatment that would be penalised today. Having the mental strength to play against someone like Peter Storey and win out through skill adds a different dimension to Best's abilities, but it doesn't mean the game was better for the existence of these so-called hardmen.

We only have to look at the treatment of Pelé by the Portuguese in the 1966 World Cup. If you look back at that game you will see that the Portuguese player Morais is not at all interested in the ball when he tackles Pelé, who, with typical resilience, struggles on with the ball until Morais hacks him down again. It was vicious stuff that went unpunished. Was the tournament better for the neutral when Pelé was literally kicked out of it? No. Outlawing the tackle from behind is a rule change that represents the idea that the sport is a spectacle of skill. There is always wrestling or cage fighting for those tired old voices perpetually telling us that the game was so much better when defenders were allowed to assault attackers. It wasn't.

Referees and VAR

I wasn't the easiest player to referee as I had a hot temper and could mouth off. Some referees wielded their authority lightly; others were a bit more officious. Some were easy to warm to, some were not. The simple truth though is that without referees there is no game. In my day they were essentially amateurs. At the highest level they are now paid well, but it is still a tough job, and although I am risking being called a hypocrite, unless players start having respect for referees we will be short of referees at all levels of the game.

Perhaps all first-team Premier League footballers should have a clause in their contract that they referee a youth game. They will then have an idea of how difficult the job is, and it is not made easier now by VAR. When I was a kid I could nip round the corner to get the *Sports Argus* on a Saturday, and in my memory, it would be in the shop by 5.15pm with all the results. The *Sports Argus* doesn't exist now, but if it did you would be lucky to get the Argus home by 6.30pm. Three o'clock kick-offs seem to be concluding close to 5pm. It's getting worse, and is being made worse by VAR.

I am in favour of goal-line technology but not interrupting a game for several minutes to check if a player's toe is over a line drawn on a TV screen. I am in favour of leaving decisions to the referee. They are now reasonably well paid and should be judged on performance. If a referee makes regular avoidable mistakes the authorities have the option to demote or retrain. The game is suffering as a spectator sport when fans can't celebrate a goal because they are worried about it being disallowed after another visit to Stockley Park.

They've Lost the Plot

'If a ball hits a player who has made their body unnaturally bigger, then a foul will be awarded.' The new rules on handball also specify that 'extra leeway will be permitted when the ball comes off a nearby player of if they cannot see the ball'. When the manager of a side (in this case, Steve Bruce) which has benefited from this rule change states that the rule makers 'have lost the plot', you know there is a problem.

The decision to award a penalty after handball by Eric Dier in a recent Tottenham v Newcastle game was ludicrous. It reflected badly on the rule makers, and badly on VAR. By the time the decision had been made my short, neat beard – much despised by Mr George at Leicester – had started to look like the George Best bush that he used to conceal the fattening of his face after excessive drinking. It was stated by Graeme Souness, one of the pundits, that the referee was only applying the new rule. But was he? Although the rule change indicates that it is a foul if a player makes his body unnaturally bigger, it also states that extra leeway will be given if they cannot see the ball. Dier could not see the ball.

Simulation

You may remember my conflict with Steve Williams from an earlier chapter. I headbutted him and was sent off. In an interview for a magazine I was asked who my favourite actor was. My reply was Steve Williams. Steve did make the contact look worse than it was, but I did make firm contact. These days the slightest little nuzzle with the forehead causes players to collapse like a cowboy shot dead in an old western. It makes my blood boil to see the lengths players go to in order to get opponents sent off. Referees should send the perpetrators off, but where there has been clear simulation the other guy should be sent off as well.

I met Steve on England duty. He took the seat next to mine on the team coach. His first words were, 'You're not going to headbutt me, are you?' He seemed like a good bloke, but I guess he might have been acting.

The Future

I am writing this during the COVID-19 crisis, and it is pertinent to ask whether some English clubs will survive. The EFL has predicted losses of up to £250m for its 72 clubs. Crowds only returned in very small numbers and at a limited number of grounds in December 2020, and the EFL has been desperate for support from the Premier League. In *Why England Lose*, authors Simon Kuper and Stefan Szymanski argue that very few clubs go out of business even during periods of economic depression when crowds fall. The problem with the crisis caused by COVID-19 is that there are no crowds. There is no doubt that many clubs are facing an uncertain future. A financial rescue package is being put together by the government, but any support is unlikely to cover the loss of revenue.

At a time when Tottenham are able to secure Gareth Bale on an astronomical salary, it is vital that the Premier League clubs respond to this crisis by providing as much support to EFL clubs as possible. In an article in *The Guardian* on 25 September, Barney Ronay asserts that Bale could keep every club in League Two in business by paying their total combined wage bill out of his annual playing salary. In the Premier League and in many EFL clubs, too much of the revenue is going on players' wages.

I am also of the view that it is time to insist that a certain proportion of players in the Premier League should be British. In the NASL three American or Canadian players had to be on the pitch for each side at any one time. The standard criticism of such a measure is that the standard in the Premier League would decline in quality. I recognise this, but when young English players like Jadon Sancho and Jude Bellingham have to go abroad to get game time at the top level, there is something wrong. You may detect an element of hypocrisy here, in that I went abroad to get game time as a young player, and as you have read, it improved all aspects of my game. It is also true that I learned from playing and training with great players. I am sure that Phil Foden has learned a great deal from David Silva and Kevin De Bruyne, but if the England team is ever to compete at the highest level, the likes of Foden need game time.

10

Heroes and Villans (Not Baddies, Not Villains)

Feeling the Blood Shiver – Bruce Springsteen

I love music and can be a little obsessive about artists and bands that I like. I have seen Springsteen 60 times. When I married Kirsty I asked her if we could both take the name Springsteen. She declined. I did change my name and took my mother's maiden name, Evans – and behind this change of name is another story. As I pointed out earlier, my dad left home when I was 16, and although he did make contact I decided that I didn't want to see him. The years had passed, and to be perfectly honest he was never a big part of my life. He may well still be alive, and I did hear that he had remarried and had children. I don't want to hurt anybody's feelings but Den and Dave were my father figures. Their surname is Evans and, when Kirsty decided against Springsteen, we became Mr and Mrs Evans.

A tenuous approach to the Boss, but I am there now. Garry Thompson introduced me to Springsteen by lending me his album, *The River*. I loved it, and recalling that I had missed the opportunity to see him in America, vowed to attend a live Springsteen concert at the earliest opportunity. Of all places, that chance came at Villa Park. Back-track 14 years and recall the young footballer testing his recovery from injury and collapsing on the driveway of Aston Hall. Move forward to the hour before the Springsteen concert, and you would have found a retired footballer drinking cans of lager adjacent to the spot where he had collapsed. They had refused me entry to Villa Park because I was carrying lager. All I wanted to do was to drink it and lose myself in the music. I did lose myself in the concert. I know it sounds pretentious, but it felt like a life-changing experience.

I don't read poetry, maybe I should, but the lyrics of Springsteen's songs always seem to speak to me. 'Independence Day' is about a troubled relationship between a father and son. It does not provide an exact parallel to my relationship with my dad and in truth, there was never much of a relationship there, especially during my teenage years. I did, though, feel a sense of liberation and independence when he left home. 'The darkness in the house has got the best of us,' goes the track, and through my 16-year-old eyes the darkness was caused by my dad.

I have always been protective of my mum, and I hated to hear her getting upset during their rows. When he left I suppose I felt that I could look to the future and so could she. It felt like independence day and I could focus on my football without worrying about my mum getting upset by my dad. Of course, in the song it is the son who leaves home, but I found as with so many Springsteen numbers I could identify with the narrator. By the way, it always felt like independence day when I left Ron Saunders behind, but I don't think Bruce had Ron in mind.

'The River' is about a man who loses his job and is struggling financially. I had lost my main job when I saw Bruce for the first time, and the lyrics seemed relevant. I felt that I was drowning in the same river. Unlike the character in the song my dream had come true, I had become a professional footballer and played for England, but the end of that dream and the current of ordinary life felt like 'something worse' than not achieving the dream in the first place. In simple terms, I guess I was feeling sorry for myself, and in a curious way Bruce seemed to have an insight into my experiences. On that evening at Villa Park I felt alive and was immersed in his music.

During the writing of this book, Springsteen has released a new album. I bought it on the day it came out. At the time I was trying to define exactly what I missed about playing football. I had defined the 'buzz' of football as a feeling of being completely alive. Then, in the track 'Ghosts', I heard Springsteen's description of the feeling that playing live gave him, 'I can feel the blood shiver in my bones.'

In my home city, Birmingham, most working-class people were employed in factories. I never made a connection with my dad, but he was a hard worker and put food on the table. Birmingham was dominated by industry. Aston was the home of Kynoch's gun factory, Ansells brewery and Dunlop. There were many manufacturing companies in Aston, and most of my school peer group followed their fathers into the factories.

In 'Factory', Springsteen sings about the nature of factory life and the way the boredom of the work grinds people down. He respects the workers who are putting food on the table for their families but is determined not to follow that path. I guess that was a factor in my determination to make it in football. I wanted a different life. I often wonder what would have happened if my mum had not pursued Vic Crowe about my apprenticeship all those years ago.

'Factory' is a reminder of the life I escaped from, and my fears about living that life certainly influenced my decision to try to pursue a career in football after retiring from playing. Ironically it is the ordinary working life that has provided more satisfaction. I enjoy my job as a school caretaker. I still, however, think that the factory life described by Springsteen, and experienced by so many of my peers at school, was not the life for me. I am grateful to my mum and Crowe for giving me the opportunity to escape.

When my first marriage ended I went through a dark period. Sue and I had been together from a young age and I was determined to fulfil my responsibilities to the kids, but I can't dispute that I was feeling sorry for myself. 'Better Days', from Springsteen's *Lucky Town* album, is about a man who feels a wave of optimism when meeting a woman. It is about Springsteen's emotions when meeting Patti Scialfa, who became his second wife. When Springsteen writes of how meeting Patty transformed his way of looking at the world, it sums up how I felt when meeting my second wife Kirsty. I felt more optimistic about life after she came into my life.

My decision to go to America was the best career choice I could have made. It wasn't an easy decision, and Sue and I were only given five hours to make our minds up. If I listen to 'Thunder Road', on the *Born to Run* album, certain lines really ring true. The narrator is trying to persuade Mary to take a chance and come with him on an adventure. The truth is that Sue didn't take a great deal of persuading, although she found it difficult to leave her family behind. Nevertheless, when Springsteen sings, 'Come take my hand, we're riding out tonight to case the promised land,' it always has echoes of the particular night we decided to commit to going to New York. The narrator tries to persuade Mary by saying, 'There's magic in the night.'

I have explained that for Sue, in that first year, there was precious little magic. The magic for me was on the pitch. The narrator in 'Thunder Road' is seizing the day, 'pulling out of here to win'. I went to New York determined to make a success of my football. I would never have been the same player had Sue and I not made that bold decision.

A curious link emerged between my obsession with Springsteen and my football career in America. I received an e-mail from a guy called Mark Stein who collected memorabilia from the NASL. He was interested in buying team shirts and wondered if I had any to sell. When he told me that he was on tour with Bruce Springsteen and the E Street Band I suspected that I was the victim of a wind-up. Mark, who is a lovely guy, turned out to be the manager of the E Street Band drummer Max Weinberg, and as a kid had been a locker boy for the Chicago Sting.

We did exchange memorabilia, but Mark, knowing of my enthusiasm for Bruce and the band, arranged for Kirsty and me to be given a stage tour before one of the band's gigs in New York at the MetLife Stadium. We met Max, who allowed me to sit behind his drum kit, and get a feel for what it is like playing those massive gigs. It was a real thrill and another great positive to emerge from my transfer to Cosmos all those years ago. Thanks Mark. Thanks Ron. I am told they call it serendipity.

George Best

My inspiration as an aspiring footballer was George Best. I would go to the Hawthorns, when Villa were not in the First Division, and my eyes would be focused on him even when he didn't have the ball. I have read that Best also loved watching great players. In Duncan Hamilton's biography of Best, *Immortal*, he tells us that Best loved Francisco Gento, Alfredo Di Stefano, and Pelé, who he travelled to Hillsborough to watch when Santos were playing against Sheffield Wednesday. That game was in 1963, and eight years later, as you have read in the introduction, I was watching Pelé in a similarly obsessive way at Villa Park.

Apparently, Best observed Pelé making diagonal runs and would note the ease with which he dropped his shoulder. George loved the way Pelé left defenders kicking thin air. I totally identified with George because I found myself learning from Pelé in much the same way when I played and trained with him. Ironically, the player who, as a boy, I learned most from watching was George – who in turn had learned from watching the great man. George and Pelé had similar qualities. Both could accelerate rapidly from a standing start, both kept the ball close to their feet, and each had the ability to drop a shoulder and put a defender on his backside.

I loved the way Best received the ball – caressing it and then turning with it in a way that expressed pure joy. It was as though the ball made him complete. Pelé was the same; both simply loved the ball. It was fascinating the way Best would emerge with the ball when a couple of defenders, sometimes more, tried to challenge him. It would make me laugh when I saw those defenders looking behind them, incredulously, as if to say, 'What happened there?' Once Best was gone there was no stopping him; it always seemed to me that he could run with the ball just as fast as he could without it. He could accelerate with effortless grace.

Gordon Banks once said I could 'wriggle like Best'. Well, I tried, but Best must have been a total nightmare to play against. It was uncanny the way he would shape to go one way then shape to go the other, and finally he would turn back the original way. It was as if the defender was hypnotised.

Best was responsible for temporarily luring me away from the Villa, and when Manchester United reached the

European Cup Final in 1968, an 11-year-old Steve Hunt was supporting them. John Aston was the man of the match after using his speed to beat the Benfica full-back time and time again. I have just watched Best's goal in that game. Apparently he was disappointed in his performance that day, but that goal was typical Best. He nutmegged the last defender, and bamboozled the keeper, feinting to go to the left of him and chopping the ball to the keeper's right side, leaving an empty net.

It brought back the memories of watching the game at Perry Barr with my friend, John Campbell, and, of course, after it had finished, I took the ball out and tried to emulate Best's move for the goal. The keeper's desperate and futile dive into the net reminded me of when I scored against Seattle Sounders. Both keepers dived when the goals were absolute certainties. The Seattle keeper had made a big mistake and was trying to atone; Enrique, the Benfica stopper, had simply been outwitted by a genius.

I felt cheated by injury at the end of my career. The move into midfield had suited me as I had become a passing midfielder and I felt I could play at a high level in that role until reaching my mid-30s. It felt as though I had lost five years of my career. Best's career ended early because of his illness. It is absolute nonsense to talk in terms of self-destruction. George, like many footballers, was the victim of an illness called alcoholism. He was cheated by this terrible affliction and so were football fans everywhere. I often wondered what type of footballer he would have become. People forget what a brilliant passer he was, and he could easily have played as a number ten in later years.

I know there is a view that time is running out in their 30s for midfielders and strikers, and I can understand that with the hard-pressing football played today, it is going to be increasingly difficult for older players, but outstanding players see things early even if they have passed their peak. Messi and Ronaldo remain outstanding players in their 30s. I am convinced that, if it hadn't been for his illness, Best would have remained a great player well into his 30s.

Footballers who tell opponents that they are going to break their legs have no place in the game. That sort of player usually relishes the title 'hard man'. I have heard that Peter Storey would tell George that he was going to break his leg each time they met. George would take great delight in skinning him. A footballer who is simply a hard man is not a footballer. Pelé, Best, Diego Maradona, Lionel Messi and Cristiano Ronaldo are all capable of riding the crudest tackles. Brilliant footballers, but all of them hard men.

Of course, it was a different era but I can't help wondering if the mismanagement of Best was in some way responsible for the brevity of his career. Best was clearly addicted before Busby retired. In the 1968/69 season United finished 11th, and, by Best's own admission, there was not a good team spirit. Team spirit can compensate for not having world-class players. My first few years at Coventry provide evidence of that.

Of course, Busby was a great manager, but Denis Law made the point that he had lost his edge by '69. There is a feeling that the effects of Munich had taken hold, and that he was far too lenient with Best. George needed help, but he also needed to be aware that he must not let his team-mates down. There is a story in *Bestie* about George being found by Wilf McGuinness with a girl in her hotel room before an FA Cup semi-final with Leeds. McGuinness wanted to send him home, but Busby persuaded him otherwise. Apparently Best had a stinker. My old manager, Johnny Giles, who had heard about the incident, and who was playing in the opposing Leeds side, accused him of being unprofessional, saying he had 'let his mates down'. Duncan Hamilton's biography of Best is a wonderful read, but it strikes me that in trying to identify the reasons for Best's drinking (shyness, pressure, isolation, desire to forget), he is rather glossing over the fact that Best had a predisposition to drink. He had an addictive personality, and his addictions were to drink and sex. Best himself was later certain that he was the victim of a disease. He was also sure that there was a genetic element evidenced in his mother's addiction to drink.

My response, when people ask me about drinking in my day, is to say it was part of the culture. That, though, is a rather simplistic answer. Why was Best allowed to begin a descent into hell while still employed as a professional footballer? In his autobiography, Bobby Charlton writes of Best, 'If he wasn't absent from training he was late.' Charlton then goes on to say, 'Even if you worried about his prospects in the longer term, for the moment it was plain that we could not jettison such a talent.' They could have jettisoned his talent, and perhaps they should have done so. Professional footballers do not appreciate a system in which one player is treated more leniently. In my view, Dave Sexton would not have stood for it, and surely neither would Bill Shankly, Don Revie, or Revie's nemesis, Brian Clough. When I first played against George, as an awestruck 18-year-old in a reserve team game, he looked like a wild bohemian with his big bushy beard and long hair. Hamilton tells us that the beard was to hide the jowls that came from his drinking.

The words 'duty of care' come to mind. Charlton's statement ultimately implies that Best's care was not the main issue. The question asked was not whether they could find help for Best's long-term welfare but whether they could squeeze a few more good results from his genius. Best should have been offered help, and if he had declined it he should have been sacked. Best, at that age, needed to reach the point that Tony Adams did when he made his admission, 'I've got a drink problem and I need to go to a meeting of Alcoholics Anonymous.' In trying to force out of Best the remains of his unique talent United were surely facilitating his self-deception.

My memories of the young Best provided inspiration to my teenage self. That moment when I came out to play against my hero for the first time will stay with me all my life. I was at the time fanatical about The Who, who sang in one of their tracks, 'I hope I die before I get old.' That was the way he played: a young man using his God-given talents to entertain both himself and the crowd. Tomorrow doesn't matter. Best's talent is 'immortal'. I will never tire of watching his genius.

Unfortunately, the man himself was not immortal. It is often said that Best was a victim of his fans, who were always eager to buy him a drink, but the real problem was that he couldn't say no. A good friend of mine was involved in the after-dinner speaking circuit for ex-footballers. He was responsible, on one such occasion, for driving, and 'looking after', Best and Rodney Marsh. Beyond a certain point, after fans had been buying him drink after drink, my friend told me that Marsh approached him to tell him to make sure George only had water. George had been drinking white wine, and my friend made the point that Best would surely notice. Marsh indicated that George was so pissed that he wouldn't know the difference.

I was in awe of Best as a footballer, but the real tragedy was that a warm, intelligent man couldn't find a way to beat the booze. If only he could have been persuaded to say the words that changed the life of Tony Adams.

Tony Adams

You would have thought that Best's problems would have made people aware of the importance of dealing with addiction issues in sport. In 1990, Adams was imprisoned for driving a car when almost four times over the legal alcohol limit. A warning sign that he was sick and needing help? Well, it doesn't seem that way from reading his book. There is no mention of support from his club or the PFA. In fact, the message that Tony gives us is that it was 'business as usual'. Frequent drunken bouts were punctuated by brilliant defensive displays.

Like Best, Adams seems to have had a strong constitution and could play and train after drinking sessions. In the 1992/93 season, when drunk, he fell down 30 concrete steps and cut his head so badly that he needed 29 stitches. In the quarter-final of the FA Cup, immediately after that injury, Adams had a brilliant game but again indulged in the kind of denial that plagued Best and Gascoigne. 'If I was that good on the pitch, I couldn't be that bad off it,' he once said.

That season, Arsenal won the FA Cup and Adams was restored to the England team. An ankle injury meant that he couldn't make the summer tour of the US, not that he was bothered, and he admitted, 'I just wanted to be free for a few weeks of drinking.' Three years later Adams arrived at 'the most painful place I have ever been, when I came to know what alcoholics refer to as "the hideous four horsemen": terror, bewilderment, frustration, despair'.

Adams is in this book as a hero – not for his football, although clearly he was a terrific centre-half and a leader of men – but because he was able to utter those three words, 'I need help', and go on to change his life, with the help of Alcoholics Anonymous. His great legacy is not the 1989 league championship, or the many other trophies, but the clinic – Sporting Chance – he set up to help other sportsmen deal with their addictions.

Brian Little

I have made clear my feelings about being given the sack at Leicester City. I had known Brian Little for a long time, and the circumstances and manner of my dismissal still rankle. What can't be denied, however, is that Brian was a fantastic player. He is a true Villa legend. Playing off Andy Gray, he was quick and skilful, and his movement was exceptional.

I played with Garth Crooks at Albion for a short while, and his runs were brilliant. The highest praise I can give Brian was that he was Crooks's equal in that department. Brian wasn't the type to score many from outside the box, but he was a deadly finisher. He deserved more than his 15 minutes of fame for England; one cap does not tell the story of what a brilliant player he was. He also, on occasions, played as an advanced playmaker behind two strikers; a versatile and highly creative talent. Brian was forced to retire at the age of 27 through injury. He nearly joined Birmingham City at one point and I think he is one of the few Villa players whose legendary status at the club would have survived a dalliance with the enemy.

Charlie Aitken

Charlie Aitken was at Cosmos when I arrived and it was he, of course, who recommended me to the club. A one-club Villa man until he went to America, he holds the club record for first team appearances. It was a strange footballing fusion: Aitken and Giorgio Chinaglia. Charlie was my nan's favourite player. She sat in the

Witton End, and her favourite refrain was that nobody would get the better of Charlie. She was a good judge of a footballer.

Charlie was indeed Mr Reliable – a no-frills full-back, few people did get the better of him. It would have been a thrill for my nan to see me play with Charlie, who is a calm man and a gentleman. In one respect, at least, he was like my uncle Dave, because I never once heard him swear. He was, and I'm sure still is, a very kind man and a great mentor for me at Cosmos.

If you are reading this, Charlie, you were great for me in New York, and you also made my nan very happy. Thank you.

Brian Clough and Peter Taylor

When Brian Clough slapped the back of my head as I walked off the pitch, after a game against Nottingham Forest, I was in hothead mode. Nigel Clough had just gained a penalty by diving, and Forest scored it to equalise in the closing stages. I was angry with Nigel and the referee. In fact, I was having a go at the referee when I felt the slap on my head. My fists automatically clenched, but on seeing Clough's familiar face, they unclenched. I was very close to belting him, but I can only think that I simply had too much respect for the man.

I'm not sure we would have got on if he had been my manager as perhaps he would have been too authoritarian and abrasive for me; my instincts are instinctively anti-authority and, as you now know from this book, I could lose my temper easily. In football terms, however, he was just my cup of tea. In Britain he was ahead of his time. 'A team blossoms only when it has the ball,' is something straight out of the Pep Guardiola handbook, yet it was Clough who said it.

You may have gathered from this book that I am an advocate of good football played on the deck; Clough was a football evangelist in that sense. I understand when managers have to be pragmatic, according to the players they inherit, but if a footballer doesn't want the ball he's not really a footballer. Let us first focus on the Derby County side he took from the Second Division to the First Division. At this point, I should mention Peter Taylor, who had an astute eye for a player. He discovered so many of the names who graced their teams. As Jonathan Wilson tells it, in *Nobody Ever Says Thank You*, the signing of Dave Mackay was Clough's most significant at Derby. Who else but Clough and Taylor would have considered taking, by Mackay's own admission, a by-then sluggish wing-half, once of course the finest of his generation, and then playing him as a sweeping centre-half behind Roy

McFarland? Why did Clough sign Mackay? To play out from the back of course, as a midfielder Mackay could pass. Does that remind you of a certain Spanish manager at Manchester City with a penchant for turning midfielders into defenders?

Talking of sweepers who could pass, let us fast forward to the City Ground, where Clough and Taylor decided yet again that they needed a sweeper who could initiate attacks and play behind Larry Lloyd. That man was Kenny Burns, a one-time centre-forward at Birmingham, who – within a year – was such a cultured centre-back that he was named Football Writers' Player of the Year.

Bremner, Mortimer, Cowans

I cannot discuss Aston Villa greats without paying tribute to the European Cup-winning team, and reluctantly, to Ron Saunders. This was a side out of the Saunders mould; hard-working, well-balanced and tough. But Tony Barton deserves a great deal of credit for taking them over the line. It is often forgotten that, during the season they won the European Cup, Villa were not playing well and finished mid-table in the First Division.

I am going to display my credentials as an Aston Villa supporter by naming the European Cup-winning midfield in this section. If there was a model Saunders player it would be an amalgam of Dennis Mortimer and Des Bremner. I read that Des believed that Ron was ahead of his time in developing a pressing game. I played against that Villa side, and there may be some truth in this. Des never gave you an easy game and, in the modern Klopp and Guardiola manner, was brilliant at regaining possession early. Des's work rate was a major factor in the success of that Villa side. It is astonishing to me that Des won only one cap and he wasn't included in the Scotland squad which went to Spain for the 1982 World Cup. He is a little more philosophical than I was about my own omission from the England squad at the same time. He simply said that Scotland had a lot of good players. I believe, however, that if Des had been playing for a Liverpool or Celtic side that had won the European Cup he would have been nailed on to go to Spain.

Dennis Mortimer is often described as the best England player never to be capped. For me, this is approaching the subject from the wrong perspective. The pertinent question is, why was he never capped? Like Des, Dennis was a Saunders type – a box-to-box midfielder with a fantastic engine. Both Des and Dennis are Aston Villa heroes despite the fact that they also played for Birmingham City. I believe that both, however, would acknowledge that the artist in that Villa holy trinity in midfield was the great Gordon Cowans.

'This isn't rugby keeper!'

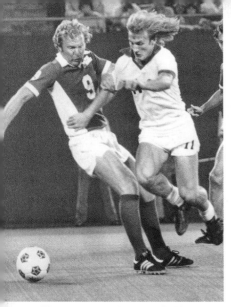

Playing against the great Bobby Moore but isn't his number upside down?!

One of the greatest players I ever faced. England should have built a team around him.

Soccer Bowl Final v Seattle at San Diego.

Early days at Coventry.

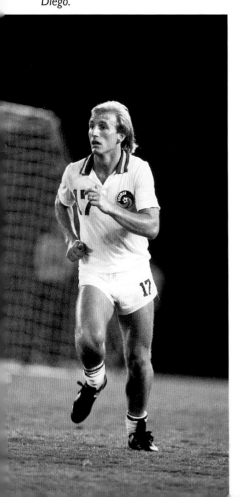

Unusually I am playing on the right here, but midfield was my natural home.

Dave Sexton was probably the best manager I worked with, a real football man.

*England debut
v Scotland at
Hampden Park.*

My second and final England cap against Russia at Wembley.

With Mark Hateley and Dave Armstrong, my ex-team-mate from Coventry and my roomie for the tour.

In front of Christ the Redeemer in Rio.

Home debut for the Baggies.

Chasing Kenny Dalglish for Albion.
It was difficult to get the ball back
against Liverpool, but my spell at
Albion was probably the best of my
career.

Bingo! We're down. The most disappointing season of my career.

'Where's your hair gone Steve?'

With Bruce Springsteen at a book signing. I'm going to reciprocate and invite him to mine.

With mighty Max, the drummer in the E Street Band.

With Kirsty on stage before the Springsteen gig.

Ask any Villa fan of a certain generation who their favourite Villa player is and the odds are that a majority will come up with Gordon. I have explained how Saunders told me, when he arrived at Albion, that he didn't want ball players in his midfield and of how my mind turned to Gordon. Gordon could pass long or short. He was a technically gifted player with great vision. Today, they would say that Gordon was a scanner, or that he saw pictures. I will simply say, in the old-fashioned way, that he played with his head up. He was a gloriously cultured player.

People sometimes ask me if I regretted leaving Villa, suggesting that if I hadn't, I might have been in that European Cup-winning side. The short answer is 'no'; Ron clearly didn't want me there and, although I had anticipated a career at Villa, after breaking into the first team, I held no great hopes of establishing myself so long as he was manager. Of course, it would have been wonderful to be part of that legendary team – especially as it was the club I had supported and grown up with – but I learned so much at Cosmos with world-class players, that I don't believe that I would have been the same player without that experience.

Dave Evans

Many professional footballers fall out of love with the game. The professional game is a different beast. The true heroes of the game are people like my uncle – Dave Evans – the joint-founder of Brantley Rovers.

I was tapped up to play for West Brom when I was watching Brantley in the local park. Acres of land full of sloping rectangles (also known as football pitches), some sloping steeply, sometimes muddy, sometimes frozen, where an assortment of men of all ages and shapes would run off the previous night's beer by imagining they were playing at Wembley. I used to love, and still do, watching Sunday league clubs gathering in the local park for pre-season training. Men full of joy, at the start of the season, simulating the stretches and warm-ups of professional footballers, only to betray, for most of them, their lack of ability when a ball comes in close proximity.

Having said that, I have seen players in park football with excellent technique. Sometimes you saw a player hit a diagonal ball 40 yards to a team-mate with a pass that Glenn Hoddle would have been proud of. Invariably, the pass would have been wasted, because his team-mate, in trying to trap the ball, would either miss it or it would bounce off leg, foot, knee or chest out to an opposing player. 'Couldn't trap a bag of cement,' as Bill Shankly once famously said about an ex-manager of mine. Both players are to be admired; the would-be Hoddle, who perhaps had harboured hopes of being 'spotted', but still turns out for the joy of stroking that diagonal ball, even though, because of his team-mate's lack of ability, it is ultimately futile. Mr Bag of Cement is also to be admired. He turns out every week hoping that one day he will channel his inner Zidane, to kill the ball on his chest with a nonchalant arching of his back. Mr Bag of Cement is like a high-handicap golfer who turns out every week because, perhaps on the 18th hole, he nailed a drive 200 yards down the fairway and thought to himself, 'Yes! That's it – I've cracked it now!'

Uncle Dave wasn't, and isn't, the typical Sunday league player. He prefers Horlicks to alcohol, having never had a drink, and has always been a very fine player. In my view, if he had specialised in football he would have been good enough for the professional game. I have an article from the *Birmingham Evening Mail* at home which I treasure as much as any article about my own career. The heading is, 'It's the Pensioner Poacher of the Penalty Area: Dave Scores at 66'. Fifty-one years after forming Brantley Rovers with his friends, Dave scored one and made one for them when he came on as sub against Northfield Hammers in the Festival League. Dave, at that time, managed Brantley – washing the kit and turning out to play when needed. On that day he had refereed in the first half and 'demonstrated how fair he is when he awarded a penalty to the opposing team'. He played, he managed, he refereed, he washed the kit, and he scored a goal at the age of 66. That's what I call a football man.

My uncles, Dave and Den, who loved football enough to instil in me, as a child, a love of the ball, are the true heroes of the game. Dave still loves the game with a passion that few professionals have. He still plays. If you happen to pass a walking football session in Aston, you may see a man in his 70s, with a neat moustache, lift his head up to make a precise pass to a team-mate. That man helped a little boy become the team-mate of the greatest player on the planet. When I started this book I would have said that George Best was my football hero. Best was in with a shout, but my all-time hero is Dave Evans.

Mrs Flash and Volunteers in Grassroots Football

In his book, *The Greatest,* Matthew Syed devotes a long passage to the role of the volunteer in sport. He writes about a man called Brian Halliday, who was chairman of Kingfisher Table Tennis Club in Woodley, near Reading, for more than 20 years. He was also chairman of the English Table Tennis Association for more than a decade. He did not receive a penny for his efforts and would not have expected to. He did it for the love of the sport, and to encourage the love of his sport in the young people of his community. It certainly worked with Syed, who played at

Kingfisher and went on to become the English table tennis number one.

It was while reading this that I decided that my uncle Dave should enter this book as a sporting hero, as an acknowledgement of his sterling work for Brantley Rovers over the course of 50 years. Through a friend I was made aware of another volunteer superhero. I have never met her, and she has a superhero name – Mrs Flash. Having arrived in inner-city Birmingham from Jamaica in the 1960s, Mrs Flash, who worked in a Birmingham hospital, realised that there were few facilities for young inner-city kids, like her two sons, to play sport. She set up a youth club on her local estate with an outdoor courtyard for football, basketball and netball. At Lea Bank Junior School, Mrs Flash organised the football. Her team won the all-Birmingham junior schools trophy three years in a row. She also ran a successful Sunday league side, and established the Little League which provided hundreds of junior school children with organised football. Many talented players emerged as a result of her efforts, some becoming professionals, and her own son Richard signed for Manchester United. Sadly his career was ended by injury.

In her red minibus, known as the Flashmobile, she would ferry talented kids to Villa and Blues for training. She would then pick up a school team for a match before returning to pick up the kids from Villa and Blues. Mrs Flash was made vice-president of the Birmingham Schools FA and given a national award by the Department for Education and Sport for her work in the community. Deservedly she received the MBE for her services for young people in Birmingham.

These achievements made me wonder if I would ever have become a professional footballer without the support of my mum, Dave, Den and my old schoolteacher, Mr Salt. Although he is not a volunteer, I must also mention Ron Wylie who first coached me in Aston Park when I was 14 and played such a large part in my career. As I say, he wasn't a volunteer, but Ron went the extra mile to help kids like me.

Mrs Flash made the opening speech at the Scarman Trust National Sports conference, attended by the then-Minister of Sport, Richard Caborn. I strongly believe that the government could be doing more, and investing more, in sport for young people, but, after this conference Mr Caborn was heard to say, 'What this country needs is more people like Mrs Flash.' 'Hear, hear,' as they say in Parliament.

For a short period I managed Cowes who played in the Wessex League. I saw at first hand how much hard, unpaid work goes into keeping Cowes going. It's remarkable to see football-loving people put in so much hard work. Cowes, being an island club, relied heavily on fundraising and sponsorship to pay for expensive trips to the mainland. I must also pay tribute to the players at Cowes who would do a shift at their jobs before playing a midweek game, often returning to the island at midnight.

Volunteers are the lifeblood of grassroots and non-league football. It is so easy to think that football is just about what happens on the pitch, but clubs like Cowes wouldn't exist without their backroom staff. I applaud the 400,000 volunteers who keep grassroots clubs alive.

11

The Big Six

ALL OVER Birmingham, in the more innocent 1960s, kids were sent out to pick up the *Sports Argus*. It would be released at about 5.15pm on a Saturday. In that *Birmingham Pink* they could read on the way home about their team. Invariably, their team would be one of what the *Argus* called the 'Big Six': Villa, Blues, Albion, Wolves, Coventry and Walsall. From our flat in Perry Barr, I could see three of their grounds – Villa Park, St Andrew's and the Hawthorns. Despite my flirtation with Manchester United, there was never any doubt where my main allegiance was to be. We were a Villa family, and when I signed for Stanley Star (aka Villa Boys), my aim was to be a Villa player.

In truth, as a child, any glamour that Villa had was connected to their glorious history in the Victorian era. Sure, they had won the FA Cup in 1957 against the Busby

Babes when I was two, but people forget that this was their first trophy for 37 years. For most of the late 1960s, when I was at Stanley Star, Villa were struggling, and when they were relegated from the First Division in '67 it is little wonder that I was attracted to the impossible glamour of Best, Charlton and Law. After three seasons in the Second Division things went from bad to worse for Villa, and at the end of 1969/70 they were relegated to the Third Division. I was 14 when this happened and was hoping to gain an apprenticeship at Villa, but even in his wildest dreams that teenage boy could not have imagined playing in the two games that preceded the club's return to the First Division. Villa had been promoted to the second tier at the end of the 1972 campaign, and I was to play in the two final games of the 1974/75 season at the end of which they returned to the promised land.

I suppose what I am saying is that the Big Six was something of a misnomer in the 1960s. It is true that Jimmy Hill had unprecedented success in leading Coventry to the First Division, but despite my affection for the club, having spent six years of my playing career there, and despite the fact that Coventry played European football in 1970/71, the real attraction of the Sky Blues was of a comparatively small club who have generally done remarkably well with little investment and against the odds.

Wolves had a glorious period in the 1950s, and brief spells of success in the '60s and '70s, before near-liquidation in the early '80s. West Bromwich Albion won the FA Cup in 1968 but they were relegated to the Second Division in 1973. A brief look at Birmingham City's honours board will confirm that they, even for the most subjective supporter, have never been a high-achieving club. Walsall are an important part of the town's identity, and it is to be hoped that in the midst of the current pandemic, clubs like the Saddlers don't go the way of Wigan Athletic, who are in administration. The fate of Wigan is a warning for all clubs below Premier League level.

As someone who played for three of the Big Six, I have long despaired about the decline of West Midlands football. It is true that Villa is my club, but I also have strong ties with Coventry, where I spent the longest spell of my career, and also with Albion, which is where I feel I played at my best. I no longer live in the area, but I know what football means to people in the West Midlands. The passions run as high as in Merseyside or Yorkshire, but the fans have suffered because of the lack of success.

I want all of the West Midlands clubs to do well. It is true that Villa won the European Cup in the 1980s, but that side was dismantled pretty quickly, and the club went into decline. I know. I was there as the sun set. The

West Midlands needs sustained success and consistent investment, but maybe there is light at the end of the tunnel.

I am writing this during the opening games of the 2020/21 season, and I am hopeful. Bear in mind, however, that I am not the world's best at making predictions. I may have egg on my face when you are reading this. Albion are struggling in the Premier League, but I am optimistic. Slaven Bilic is a good manager, they play good football and I think he can keep them up. Blues survived in the Championship, and seem to be playing with discipline under Aitor Karanka, but they do, however, need to find a better balance and score some goals. Coventry are struggling in the Championship, but they have beaten table-topping teams and they seem to have a good manager in Mark Robins. Wolves are stable in the Premier League and are more likely to win a European place than be drawn into a relegation battle. Incredibly, Villa have beaten Liverpool 7-2 and Arsenal 3-0. It was so important that Villa held on to Jack Grealish, a highly gifted player, and as fans are inclined to sing these days, 'one of our own'.

I was delighted to see Coventry gain promotion last season. I would have been even more satisfied to see the club playing in Coventry. Like any Sky Blues supporter, it breaks my heart to see the club without a home. The relegation battles I was involved in there concluded with the club staying in the top tier, but it was touch and go. If the directors of the club, those who agreed to sell Highfield Road and invested all their hopes in the Ricoh Arena, had taken part in those relegation battles, they would have learned that there are no guarantees in football. It took a lot of sweat, a bit of luck, a load of spirit, and excellent management to stay up. It could easily have gone the other way.

'We always threw everything at staying up,' said Geoffrey Robinson, a former director of the club. He was trying to explain the thinking that led to the sale of Highfield Road and the disastrous decisions that resulted in the club becoming tenants at the Ricoh Arena. The relegation that had such disastrous consequences for Coventry took place in 2001. A proper football man would have advised the board members that it was foolish to pin all their hopes on staying up. As ever, it is the supporters who suffer. The details of the disastrous Ricoh Arena project can be read in Simon Gilbert's brilliant analysis, *A Club Without A Home*.

I said I might have egg on my face. It happened sooner than I thought. Shortly after predicting that West Bromwich Albion would survive under Slaven Bilić, he was dismissed. It seems like a bad decision to me by Albion's owners and another shocking example of short-termism. Bilić took Albion up and his side had fought hard for a 1-1 draw against Manchester City in the game immediately before he was sacked. Contrast the treatment of Bilić with the trust Norwich City – now at the top of the Championship, following their relegation last season – seem to have in Daniel Farke. I do hope that this statement doesn't prove to be the kiss of death for Farke.

12

Subbuteo in the Snow: Reflections on a Friendship, by Dean Brookes

I HAVE not really properly reflected on my relationship with Steve until now. This friendship has always been there; we have known each other since the age of five. Our families knew each other as we lived in the same road as young children, and we both moved to Perry Barr with our families when we were older.

The main reason that our friendship has endured is, I think, down to trust. Like most people, I have had some dark times in my life, and Steve has always been there for me. Typically, his advice has been practical, and generally this was what I needed. As kids our friendship was cemented by common interests: football, music, dogs. I know that Steve has mentioned some of the antics we got up to as teenagers, but I'm sure he also remembers our Subbuteo battles after school (Villa fans look away) as in those days his Subbuteo team was always Manchester United.

Steve was highly competitive, and would water the Subbuteo pitch to suit his style. The battles took place at Steve's mum Joan's flat in Perry Barr where the heating was under-floor. He would dry the pitch on the floor and would claim in later years that he used under-pitch heating before Jimmy Hill. In order to add authenticity, on one occasion after a heavy snowfall we went outside to gather snow to put alongside the pitch.

Neither did snow prevent us going out for a kick-about. As young kids we played football in Steve's nan's garden. Of course I could see even then that Steve had real ability, but I think at that age our ambitions only stretched to playing for Steve's uncle Dave's side – Brantley Rovers. I am glad to report that I made more appearances for Brantley than Steve did. It is only fair to point out that he made more appearances for England. For a couple of seasons, when he was at Coventry, Steve managed Brantley. I think he derived as much pleasure from doing that as he did from professional football. I must say that being Steve's best mate sometimes did me no favours when it came to his selection of the Brantley side – inexplicably on several occasions he made me substitute.

For one game I was Steve's manager. I ran a side called Ajax in the Birmingham Over-35 League, and when we reached the cup final I asked Steve to play. By that time he had retired and was living with his second wife, Kirsty. As you know his knee was pretty well shot away. I probably shouldn't really have asked, but I think he wanted to do me a favour. He said he would be sub, and that he would come on if we needed him. Bizarrely, he came on for another international player, who had represented the Faroe Islands.

Bad knee or not, Steve scored one and made another, in this way he replicated his contribution to Pelé's finale. This was Steve's final competitive game – rather a contrast to Pelé's last match against the Seattle Sounders. I did ask Steve if he thought Pelé might repay the favour, but I suppose registering Pelé in the Birmingham Over-35 League might have raised a few eyebrows. In fact, when Steve came on, it caused a bit of a stir in the opposition ranks. We had registered him as Steve Evans – perfectly legitimate as that was what he had changed his name to – but there were several Villa fans on the opposing side. They recognised him, and I'm not sure they were altogether happy to find themselves on the opposing team.

Another person who wasn't very happy was Kirsty. The game didn't do Steve's knee much good, and I think she thought I had prioritised managerial glory over his physical condition. She was right. Sorry, Kirsty.

I know that Steve has spoken about our shared love of music, and of how Dave generously paid for us both to see concerts by a galaxy of rock stars. Both football and music provided colour, and escape from what then appeared to be the rather grey environment of inner-city Birmingham. Football and music brought a bit of glamour into our lives.

I suppose it is a measure of how genuine our friendship is that although I may have envied his ability, I was never jealous of his success. Steve's entry into the world of professional football, and in particular his move to Cosmos, gave me vicarious pleasure and sprinkled me with a touch of the glamour. During the Cosmos years I didn't see as much of Steve, but knowing that your best mate – the one you had spent hours kicking a ball with – was a team-mate of Pelé seemed at times too fantastic to be true. It honestly didn't seem an enormously long time between the Subbuteo years and Steve's Cosmos years. One minute Steve's playing Subbuteo with Dean Brookes, the next, he's making goals for Pelé, who, in our childhood in Brum, was as exotic and exalted as any sporting hero could possibly be.

On a visit to Brum from New York, Steve suggested we go for a drink. It was a surprise when we went into a hotel rather than a pub. We were sitting by the bar when a man I vaguely recognised walked to our table. It turned out to be Gordon Milne, who was there to agree the final conditions of Steve's contract. Steve had kept this quiet. I think he knew it would mean a lot to me that he would be back in Brum and was about to sign for Coventry.

I hardly missed a Coventry game; typically Steve always included me. I would meet him in the players' lounge after the game, usually with his mum Joan and uncle Den, and then Steve and I would generally go for a drink afterwards. I was always a big Liverpool fan and it was after a Coventry–Southampton game that I felt a tap on my shoulder; I turned around to see my football hero, Kevin Keegan. Steve had set him up to give me a surprise. They say you shouldn't meet your heroes but Kevin was charm itself, telling me and Joan how highly he rated Steve. In the years that Steve was at Coventry that young side could be inconsistent, but, despite a tricky start, I hope I am not being too subjective in saying that Steve maintained a consistently high level of performance. In my view, he was one of the best left-sided midfield players in the country.

Our love of music nearly had unfortunate consequences for us both on an eventful evening in Palm Springs. It is a curious story that wouldn't have happened if I hadn't had a mate who had played for Cosmos. I was in Long Beach, California, with work; Steve was in Palm Springs with

Kirsty on holiday. It happened to be my 41st birthday, and I had bumped into a chap called Wassel Bodnar who had been a huge fan of Cosmos. Over a drink I told Wassel about my friendship with Steve and discovered that Steve was one of his favourite players. I told him that Steve was in Palm Springs. Wassel wanted to meet him and told me that he would drive me up there. After a quick phone call to Steve I found myself in Wassel's car accompanying him on the 113-mile drive to Palm Springs. After 90 minutes of Cosmos chat with Steve, Wassel went back to California.

Kirsty suggested that Steve and I should have a boys' night out to celebrate my birthday. It could well have been my last birthday. As usual, we looked for a bit of live music and happened on a small Palm Springs bar with a pretty decent rock bank holding forth. I hadn't really noticed a gang of rednecks in the bar until one of them approached Steve. Something told me that this guy was not a Cosmos fan looking for an autograph. Steve later told me that his exact words were, 'We don't like faggots here.' Steve is a tough bloke, but this guy was enormous, and my trouble sensor was on high alert. I could see the rest of the redneck group tensing for action. I had a word with the barman who acted quickly and phoned the police. I must give full credit to the Palm Springs police. They arrived within two or three minutes to dispatch the culprits to the local prison.

I returned to Long Beach the following day and probably experienced as much fear in the propeller plane as I did from the angry giants in the bar. I can't say my short stay in Palm Springs wasn't a terrifying experience, but my 41st birthday had been an adventure directly as a result of the fame of my oldest friend.

Steve was never Billy Big Time, and, though he is essentially very private, to those he trusts he is loyal and inclusive. He always got me in to the Christmas parties at Coventry, Albion and Villa. On one occasion I arrived at a Villa fancy dress party in a pig outfit. I spent the evening chatting to famous footballers like Andy Gray, and I was drinking beer through my nostrils – a process which undoubtedly contributed to my inebriation. Steve woke me up in the spare room of his house the following morning. I was still wearing the pig costume.

I know that Steve has confessed that he is not a forgiving character. He is loyal to those he trusts, but his experiences at the end of his career, and in retirement, have meant that this aspect of his character has become more pronounced. He will not tolerate an abuse of trust, and I know that since retirement he has felt let down by people he regarded as friends.

I can't conclude this section without giving thanks from me, and on Steve's behalf, to all those who assisted with his benefit year. I organised it, but I couldn't have done it without Abdul Rashid, Steve Rochester, John Mewis, Nicky Platts, Ted and Mick Halpin, Cuz Gaz and the Jock, and Bill Lewis.

I felt proud watching my friend play at the highest level, but I would have been proud to be his mate if he had spent his working life in a factory.

I have only one complaint – Steve, why did you put me on the bench for Brantley?

13

It's Worth a Try

I WAS grateful for Dean's intervention in that bar, but he has neglected to tell you about the incident that preceded it. After dinner, Kirsty, Dean and I went to a British bar. Behind the counter were the four national flags of the union. In a fit of English nationalism, Dean turned to the barman and told him he could dispense with the Scottish, Northern Ireland and Welsh flags, as the flag of St George, was, according to my old friend, the only one that mattered. Looking for support from a group of blokes, the only other customers, Dean urged them to back him up. In broad accents they replied that they couldn't do that because they were Welsh. Fortunately they were rather more benign than the rednecks we encountered later that evening. I did have a flashback to the very angry Scots who confronted the England coach on the way to Hampden. I'm not sure that they would have been as tolerant. Why Dean had assumed they were English I don't know.

There is another story connected to Dean that I must include. I was Dean's best man at his wedding on 12 November 1982. It took place on a Friday because I was due to play for Coventry against Liverpool on the Saturday. Dean had hired top hats and tails for the occasion and they weren't due to be returned until the Monday. I am essentially a private and reserved person, but I am occasionally tempted to indulge in the odd theatrical gesture, so I arrived at Anfield in my top hat and tails. My team-mates bet me that I wouldn't wear the wedding gear while inspecting the pitch. So it was that I found myself in front of the Kop tipping my top hat to some of the most passionate fans in the world. They responded with what I can only describe as typical Scouse humour, and their comments weren't understated. I am pleased to say, however, that on the conclusion of my performance the Liverpool supporters gave me a rousing ovation. I may as well have played in my wedding gear; we lost 4-0.

I want to pay tribute to the family and friends who have supported me in my career. As I said in the first chapter, I could not have had a more supportive mother – and her brothers, Dave, and the late Den, have been absolute rocks for me.

I must pay tribute to my first wife, Sue, who was my childhood sweetheart, and has been a wonderful mother to my children. My sons Simon and Jonathan are chalk and cheese, but they are very close. Simon has strong opinions and is not slow to express them; Jonathan is more laid-back in his personality. By the way Jon, if you are reading this, I hope you have lifted the ban you imposed on your brother at your pub. Apparently Simon was disturbing the locals with his vociferous support during a televised Villa game. Jon is married to Laura and has two children, Harley and Kiara. Both boys love Villa and Oasis in equal measure. My daughter Natalie is also a great source of pride – she is a great full-time mother to George and to twin girls, Holly and Sophie. She is married to Dave. I love meeting up with my children, their partners and my grandchildren.

I am including Dean as an honorary member of my family as we are like brothers, and have been mates since the age of five. He has always been a great support. I am not a social person, but I value Dean's friendship. He is even-tempered, with a calm nature, and he is great fun to be with. I have been with Kirsty my wife for 28 years, and married for 25. I will be forever grateful for her love and support, and my love for Kirsty is at the centre of my life. She has supported me through some dark times. And at last I think she may have guided me to healthy maturity.

I cannot conclude the book without a reference to my love of dogs. You may recall that my strange Van Gogh appearance, with a bandaged ear, when I arrived in America to meet my new team-mates, was as a result of playing with my friend's dog. In a strange way, what I love about them reflects my own major flaw. They are forgiving creatures, and never hold a grudge. It has been said before but I have found dogs to be better friends than most humans. I sometimes think that I would like to hear what my dog Barney has to say, but ultimately I value the fact that I can talk to him in total confidence. Before Barney I had Bruce (no prizes for guessing who he was named after), and Pepper, but they died within months of each other. It took me a long while to get over their deaths.

The driving force in my career has always been the desire to prove myself at the top level. It is difficult sometimes for professional footballers to accept that football is just a game, and that nobody dies after a defeat or relegation. It takes some of us footballers a long time to grow up. I am the type of person who, even after difficult events, just tries to get on with my life. I am not especially reflective, and do not enjoy thinking about painful experiences, but writing this book has made me reflect on the issues I had consigned to the further recesses of my consciousness. My dad left a note the size of a Post-It on the kitchen table announcing his departure. I have deliberately tried to avoid reflecting on why I rejected his attempt to meet me.

Recently I received a letter and some photographs from my cousin, Joanne. One showed me as a boy of ten on my dad's shoulders on the beach at Weymouth. I looked happy; he looked happy. Perhaps I have deliberately ignored my happy times with him, because I can only recall the sense of relief both for myself, and for my mum, when he did leave. I don't know fully what went on between my mum and my dad – what child does? All I know is that my natural instincts were to side with my mum. The pictures did make me think about why I didn't feel a bond with him; after all he liked football, and by the time he left I was on the brink of my apprenticeship at Villa, and had been attached to Villa since the age of 11. Why didn't we bond over Pelé's beautiful game? I cannot understand why he appeared to show such little interest in me as a teenager. I can't understand why he took so long to make contact.

I probably rejected his invitation to meet him partly out of consideration for my mum, but also because I was so focused on my own football. Was he so sensitive that my failure to contact him put him off having another go? I feel as a father that if I had been in his position I would have tried again. The pictures sent by my cousin made me feel sad. Like most men of my generation I am not openly sensitive or emotional, but I sometimes wonder whether he ever watched me from the terraces or on television. Did he see me collect the goal of the season award from Jimmy Greaves? Did he ever see my goal in Pelé's final game? Did he see me run out at Hampden or Wembley in an England shirt? Mostly, though, I feel sad that in that short Post-It note he cut himself off from contact with his future grandchildren. I know that in not responding to his invitation to meet him I was partly responsible for that, but to try only once?

Perhaps he is still alive. He would be in his 80s now. Perhaps he married again and had a new family. I did hear that he moved to Redditch, and I suppose there is a vague possibility that if he is still alive, or if he has a wife and children who are still alive, that he or they might read this book. Time has passed and I am 64 now. At one time I would have said I didn't care what happened to him, but I hope now that he had a happy life. Perhaps I am becoming more forgiving as I get older.

I have been reading *Fever Pitch* by Nick Hornby. He writes about the separation of his parents, and of how in an attempt to bond with him, his father would suggest trips to the theatre, rugby matches and motor racing. Nick wasn't interested in any of these pursuits, but eventually they bonded over football and their support of Arsenal. Reading this makes me even more mystified about why my dad, who played and liked football, never attempted to bond with me over my great passion.

I guess a psychoanalyst would say that changing my name was essentially a rejection of my father, but I think there was also the 'fresh start' factor. I had felt let down by professional football; I was marrying again and felt as though I was starting a new life – especially when we moved to the Isle of Wight. On the island I did remain in touch with the game by coaching kids, and I managed Cowes for a while. In truth though, as Steve Evans I felt free to escape the football bubble, and I embraced a working life outside the game. I finally realised I could be part of a team; I could do a day's work and not worry about the fickle nature of the professional game. I never felt, as Billy Kee did, that I wanted to stop playing. My drive to succeed in the game was such a powerful force that it became a massive obsession. I don't regret that – it stood me in good stead as a player. I was always determined to improve, and I believe I gave everything. If you are playing at the top level, week in and week out, the obsessive nature of the game can freeze your emotional development and undermine your appreciation of 'ordinary life'.

As Steve Evans, I have come to realise why Billy Kee came to his decision to retire at the age of 29. It took me too long to realise that there is life outside football.

It is appropriate that shortly before this book was concluded, Pelé celebrated his 80th birthday. Despite a career played almost entirely in the top tier of English football, despite winning two England caps, my season with Pelé is the topic that most people want to hear about. I don't mind; it was a privilege to play with him. My own thoughts are now turning to my retirement from my school caretaking job. I plan to finish in about 18 months. What will I do then? Well as a young footballer said, when asked that question by a football magazine reporter, 'I'd better start thinking about that.'

In his autobiography, Arsène Wenger speculates on what God might say when he gets to the pearly gates. Arsène wondered if God might think he had wasted his life simply trying to win games of football. '"That's all?" he'll probably ask, disappointed.' I'm not sure whether Giorgio Chinaglia is in God's heaven, and I'm not sure he would support my application anyway. Surely Warner Communications have some clout. I never used the phrase to gain entrance to Studio 54, but I might simply say, 'I'm with the Cosmos.' It's worth a try.

Bibliography

Adams, T., *Addicted* (HarperCollins, 1998)

Brearley, M., *On Form* (Little, Brown, 2017)

Calvin, M., *No Hunger in Paradise. The Players. The Journey. The Dream* (Arrow Books, 2017)

Cox, M., *Zonal Marking* (HarperCollins, 2019)

Ferguson, A., *Leading* (Hodder & Stoughton, 2016)

Gascoigne, P., *My Story* (Headline Publishing, 2004)

Gernon, A., *Retired. What Happens to Footballers When the Game's Up* (Pitch Publishing, 2016)

Gilbert, S., *Coventry City, A Club Without a Home* (Pitch Publishing, 2016)

Giles, J., *A Football Man. The Autobiography* (Hachette Books Ireland, 2010)

Hamilton, D., *George Best, Immortal. The Approved Biography.* (Windmill Books, 2014)

Harris, H., *Pelé. His Life and Times* (Robson Books, 2001)

Heskey, E., *Even Heskey Scored* (Pitch Publishing, 2019)

Hill, J., *The Jimmy Hill Story. My Autobiography* (Hodder & Stoughton, 1998)

Hopcraft, A., *The Football Man, People and Passions in Soccer* (Aurum Press, 2006)

Hughes, C., *The Winning Formula* (Collins, 1990)

Keegan, K., *Kevin Keegan. My Life in Football* (Macmillan, 2018)

Kuper, S. and Szymanski, S., *Why England Lose & Other Curious Football Phenomena Explained* (HarperSport, 2010)

Newsham, G., *Once in a Lifetime. The Extraordinary Story of the New York Cosmos* (Atlantic Books, 2006)

Pelé, *My Life and the Beautiful Game* (Doubleday, 1977)

Pelé, *The Autobiography* (Pocket Books, 2007)

Perarnau, M., *Pep Confidential: The Inside Story of Pep Guardiola's First Season at Bayern Munich* (ArenaSport, 2014)

Phelps, S., *29 Minutes from Wembley. The Inside Story of Coventry City's 1980/81 Season* (Pitch Publishing, 2017)

Plenderleith, I., *Rock'n'Roll Soccer. The Short Life and Fast Times of the North American Soccer League* (Icon Books, 2014)

Risoli, M., *Arrivederci Swansea. The Giorgio Chinaglia Story* (Mainstream Publishing Company, 2000)

Roberts, B., *Bottled. English Football's Boozy Story.* (Pitch Publishing, 2019)

Robson, B., *An Englishman Abroad. My Autobiography* (Macmillan, 1998)

Steen, R., *The Mavericks. English Football When Flair Wore Flares* (Bloomsbury, 1994)

Stiles, N., *Nobby Stiles, After the Ball. My Autobiography* (Hodder & Stoughton, 2003)

Sydenham, R., *Ticket to the Moon. Aston Villa. The Rise and Fall of a European Champion* (deCoubertin Books, 2019)

Syed., M. *The Greatest. The Quest for Sporting Perfection* (John Murray Publishers, 2017)

Symynkywicz, J.B., *The Gospel According to Bruce Springsteen* (Westminster JohnKnox Press, 2008)

Tate, T., *Girls With Balls. The Secret History of Women's Football* (John Blake Publishing, 2013)

Wenger, A., *My Life in Red and White. My Autobiography* (Weidenfeld & Nicolson, 2010)

Wilson, J., *Nobody Ever Says Thank You. Brian Clough. The Biography* (Orion Books, 2011)

Also available at all good book stores

9781785316470

9781785313929

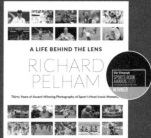

9781785315466

9781785315213

9781909626621

9781785313035

9781785315534

9781785310379

9781785318382